Asian Mythology

A Captivating Guide to Chinese Mythology, Japanese Mythology and Hindu Mythology

Free Bonus from Captivating History (Available for a Limited time)

Hi History Lovers!

Now you have a chance to join our exclusive history list so you can get your first history ebook for free as well as discounts and a potential to get more history books for free! Simply visit the link below to join.

Captivatinghistory.com/ebook

Also, make sure to follow us on:

Twitter: @Captivhistory

Facebook: Captivating History:@captivatinghistory

Contents

Part 1: Chinese Mythology

A Captivating Guide to Chinese Folklore Including Fairy Tales, Myths, and Legends from Ancient China

Introduction

Chinese mythology is a wealth of treasure composed of multiple religions, people groups, regions, and ideas. Perhaps the word *mythologies* would be more accurate than mythology, as it really encompasses so many different pantheons.

China, being a large and ancient country, also has a large and ancient tradition of mythology, legends, and folktales. Long ago, tales traveled orally and shifted in each region to be appropriate to the people's landscape, ideas, and beliefs. This means that each story or myth often has numerous versions with slightly different emphasis. In this book, these versions sometimes favor one over another and other times have been combined, but either way, this book will give you a taste of the vast realm that is Chinese mythology.

You will encounter tales of the immortals, people who have managed to contribute to or do something so special that Heaven itself decided to bless them with eternal life. In other cases, like that of the Monkey King, immortality was taken through cunning and skill. A select few, like Nüwa and the Jade Emperor, were immortals from the very beginning. Gods are also much more tangible in Chinese mythology and are even considered fallible. Even Lao Tzu, founder of Taoism, loses his perfection with the rise of Buddhism, and Buddha becomes the new infallible immortal and the exception to this rule. Though equality to the gods was attainable, and sought after, it was nothing to take for granted. Gods were highly respected and feared and many had an altar in their homes dedicated to a certain god or their ancestors.

China is an ancient and proud country for good reasons. Many of their myths, legends, and folktales are highly respected and read even today. If you are ready to be captivated by this multitude of mythologies, then snakes, spirits, demons, dragons, phoenixes, immortals, and mere mortals all await you in the pages to come.

Chapter 1 – The Origin of Earth and Humans

In the cosmic chaos, there was an egg. Inside the egg lay Pangu. He was the first god, the first giant, and simply first. Laying inside the egg, he began to form heaven and earth. Every day he would grow, and every day the heavens would rise ten feet higher and the earth would grow ten feet thicker. In the beginning, it was small and chaos still ensued all around. But each day as Pangu grew so did heaven and earth. After 18,000 years, Pangu was finally finished. Heaven was now extremely high and the earth was incredibly deep. Some say this was the formation of Yin (turbid Earth) and Yang (limpid heaven), while others would say that Yin and Yang came first, putting order into the earth and that it was only from that order Pangu first began to grow and eventually emerge.

As all things, except immortals, must die, so did also Pangu. But with his death, creation bloomed. For his body became everything we see around us. His left eye became the sun, while his right became the moon. From the strands of his beard, the stars were formed. His four limbs and five extremities became the edges of the earth and the Five Mountains. His blood formed the rivers, while his breath became the wind and clouds. His flesh turned to earth and the hairs on his head became the plants and trees to grow in it. Metals and rocks appeared from his teeth and bones, while his semen and marrow became jade and pearls. Finally, his sweat and fluids gave the earth rain so that it could hold life. Perhaps Pangu was also covered in mites and insects and it was them that became the first humans, but on that point, Nüwa would like to disagree.

The goddess Nüwa saw the earth and heaven that Pangu had formed with his dying body and his final breath. She found it so beautiful that she decided to live there. But after a while, she became lonely and decided to make people. She took up the yellow earth and began to form the people with her hands. The work was tiring and exhausted her. Eventually, she decided to grab a leather cord and simply drag it through the earth, shaking off the pieces of earth from it and creating the rest of the people that way. Now she no longer had to be alone. But after a while, the humans began to die so Nüwa started to form new people again. She knew she could not be bothered to keep forming new people constantly, so instead she gave humans a way to reproduce. After this, she withdrew, being content with what she had made. Little did she know that her work was not done yet.

Many years later, a terrible flood passed over the entire land and only two people survived, a brother and a sister. Both of them wanted to reproduce and ensure that humanity would survive, however, they felt great shame because they knew they were siblings and should not intertwine. They called to the heavens, but received no answer, so they decided to do two tests. First, they went up a high mountain, rolling down two millstones, one on each side of the mountain. Only if the stones landed next to each other could they then marry. The stones rolled down the height of the mountain, and at the bottom, both were lying next to each other. They had passed the first test and now felt comfortable getting married. Now, they went to separate locations and made fires. If the smoke from the fires intertwined with each other, they could have children and would be able to repopulate the desolate earth. After the fires had been made, both the brother and sister looked up into the sky. Slowly, the smoke that had risen separately from both their fires had become one. The brother and sister were sure they had the blessings of heaven and so they had children. However, when the sister finally gave birth, it was not the child they had expected. Instead, a spherical piece of flesh had been born. They were distraught. Had they misread the signs? For nine months they had waited for a child and instead received this abomination. They wept together, and as they wept, Nüwa heard them and appeared before them. She took a knife and cut open the spherical piece of flesh and formed not one child but many.

After humanity had been created and was reproducing, the Jade Emperor, Lord of Heaven, sent three emperors to rule over them. The first he sent was "Tian Guan," meaning ruler of heaven. He would bring them happiness, freedom, and riches. The second was "Di Guan," the ruler of earth, who would judge over the people and their actions. The third was "Shui Guan," the emperor of water, who would control the rivers and overcome diseases. These three emperors were worshipped over all of China.

When the Jade Emperor saw humans on earth and how they were living, he decided to give them some rules on food. He called to him the dung beetle and told it to tell the humans to eat once every three days. However, by the time the dung beetle had traveled back down to the humans, he had confused the message and instead told the humans to eat three times a day. The humans feasted away, gorging themselves with food, and as a result began to excrete a vast amount. At this time, Earth and Heaven were closely linked, held together by great pillars. The Jade Emperor was horrified by how revolting the humans were and could not stand the stench, so he separated Heaven and Earth to get away from the smell. To punish the beetle, he made it eat the dung that the humans excreted.

Author's Comment:

In this section, many creation myths have been fused, when often Pangu would be its own answer to the "Creation" question, and Nüwa would be another. With the creation of the humans, the brother and sister myth often does not co-exist with Nüwa, and in some versions they simply do one test and everything works out. Another version, not included here, has a giant snake give birth to all animals and then finally humans. This said, creation myths are not a dominating aspect of Chinese Mythology and there are not as many records of them as there are of other areas (like the creation of the immortals and various arts or ideas) – it seems like the origin of the human race and Earth was not as important of a question to the ancient Chinese.

The Jade Emperor is, along with Nüwa, one of the few immortals who simply exists and has no creation. Chinese mythology is filled with emperors, some which are based on real historical emperors who have been mythologized and others who simply are gods that are called 'emperors'. All of China's emperors were seen as gods, just as the Pharaohs in Egypt where. But it can be very hard to determine which emperors were gods of mythology and which were based on historical rulers. The Jade Emperor is always in Heaven and portrayed as the ruler of all the gods in Taoist mythology.

Chapter 2 – Writing and Art

Cang Jie

Huang Di, the Yellow Emperor, one of the foremost legendary rulers in ancient China, had a historiographer named Cangjie. Cangjie's role was to record everything that happened in the land. Since writing didn't exist, Cangjie used ropes of various lengths and colours to memorize every event and experience. Now, Cangjie had been born with four eyes and was incredibly gifted, but eventually even he found it difficult to remember what each piece of rope meant. He knew he had to find a new method to record history. Prostrating himself before the emperor, he asked for some time off from his duties to devise a new technique to remember everything.

Cangjie set out from the palace, meeting with people from all over the land for inspiration. He spent months following creatures, studying their shapes, signs, and patterns. After traveling across the land and studying nature and society, Cangjie finally settled down in a secluded cave, away from everything. There he began to note down symbols that reflected their character. For example, the pictograph for sun followed the sun's round shape, while the moon showed off its crescent phase. The word "field" illustrated the layering of the rice paddies. He invented a character for everything and there were as many characters as grains of rice in all of China. After Cangjie had finished his great work of inventing a written language, he set out to teach everyone. However, no one could remember all of the characters that he taught. Even Confucius himself only learned seventy percent of the original amount. When Cangjie realized that even China's most intelligent scholars could not learn all of his symbols and pictographs, he was frustrated and angry. He threw the other thirty percent away to all the other foreign countries in the world, giving them a method of writing and remembering.

When Nüwa saw the pictographs that Cangjie had created, she was angry. The character for "nü," meaning "female," an intrinsic part of Nüwa's very essence and name, had been used in numerous other characters that had negative connotations. Nüwa confronted Cangjie.

"Cangjie, do you look down on women? Thinking that our character reflects words like demon and wicked?"

Cangjie recoiled from the accusations and apologized deeply to the mother of humans. Nüwa watched and waited as he picked up his brush and set to work on a few new characters. After this, both "good" and "mother" were created with the character "nü" as a part of them.

Ma Liang and the Paintbrush

In a poor village there lived a poor boy. The boy was called Ma Liang, and he loved to draw and paint. Everywhere he went he would find a way to draw. Sometimes he would use a stick in the sand and other times he would manage to find a piece of charcoal. He became very good at drawing, so good that some said his drawings could be mistaken for real things. Despite his skill, he continued to be poor and found that his drawings could not help the other poor villagers either.

Then one night, he had a dream. An old man visited him with a beautiful paintbrush. Ma Liang had never owned a paintbrush and knew that with it he could paint marvelous things. The old man approached him and handed him the brush. "I have seen your noble heart. Use this brush to help people."

When Ma Liang woke up, the paintbrush was lying next to him. The dream had been real. But how would the paintbrush help people? Besides, he had no paint to go with it. He picked up the paintbrush and examined it. It had a beautiful mahogany handle and the brush itself was exquisitely delicate. He began to paint in the air, swishing the brush carefully as if he was painting. Suddenly, the dog that he had outlined in the air appeared and started to bark. He painted a bone on his wall, the brush adding its own colors and shadows where needed. The dog took the bone happily and ran out of Ma Liang's little hut. Ma Liang wasted no time and started to paint food, all of it becoming real.

Ma Liang headed out into the village where he knew the need was great and had heard the farmers complaining about the lack of water. He set out to the outskirts of the village and painted a river which roared to life. When the farmers heard of what he had done, they were overjoyed and thanked him. Now they could fetch water for their crops from the river. But Ma Liang knew that the crops would take time to grow and saw that many families were starving now, so he painted bowls of food for them and made sure that they could all make it to the next harvest.

After this, he set out to the next village and traveled over all of China, helping each place with what they needed.

His fame grew with his extensive travels and soon the emperor had heard of the boy with the magic paintbrush. The emperor called on Ma Liang to visit him as he wanted to personally thank Ma Liang for his services to the land.

Ma Liang knew there were still many villages to visit and lots of people who were still in need of his help, but he could not refuse the call of the emperor, so he headed to the palace and appeared before the ruler of China.

Appearing before the emperor, Ma Liang bowed low, barely having time to register the emperor's command of "Seize him!" Guards grabbed him, took his paintbrush, and threw him in prison.

The emperor was pleased to finally have the magic paintbrush in his possession. Now he could create anything he wanted. He began by drawing a large pile of gold, but nothing happened. No gold appeared. The emperor called upon his most famed artists and painters, but none of them could make anything appear out of the paintbrush. Finally, the emperor gave up, realizing that only Ma Liang would be able to wield the paintbrush. He brought the boy back to court, still in his shackles.

"If you draw for me what I ask for, I will set you free," the emperor said.

Ma Liang saw his precious paintbrush and longed to have it back. All the farmers and poor people in the land flashed through his mind. He had no desire to help a greedy emperor, but knew that without his paintbrush, he would rot in prison. "What would you like me to draw?" he asked.

"I want a mountain of gold where I can always go to get more gold."

Ma Liang was unshackled and handed the paintbrush. He began to draw, but instead of a mountain, he drew the sea.

"Why did you draw the sea? I want a mountain of gold. Not a sea." The emperor was furious and seemed tempted to throw Ma Liang back into prison.

Ma Liang quickly began to draw a mountain in the middle of the sea and filled it with enormous piles of gold. The fury in the emperor quickly subsided, replaced by a hunger shining bright in his eyes.

"Quickly!" he said. "Draw me a ship so I can collect the gold!"

Ma Liang agreed and painted the emperor a ship.

The emperor wasted no time and jumped on the ship, ordering his men to follow. As soon as they were out at sea, Ma Liang added wind and a great storm rose up. The storm became more violent as Ma Liang only added to the large waves that were brewing. They threw the ship back and forth until one huge wave crashed over it, sinking it to the bottom of the sea.

With that, the land was rid of the greedy emperor and Ma Liang set out to help the poor again. The new emperor was benevolent to Ma Liang and supported his cause, and Ma Liang and his magic paintbrush were loved by everyone in the land.

Ling Lun

Ling Lun was chosen to be the minister of music by the Jade Emperor who ordered him to invent and make music. Ling Lun thought about it and then set out to a nearby mountain. He walked around and saw many bamboo shoots. Taking one of them, he carved it into a thin pipe. He carved five holes into it and created five notes. It was a good start, and the notes were clear and different.

A phoenix was flying above him, singing its beautiful song. Ling Lun's little pipe was nothing in comparison to the marvel of the phoenix song and he wanted to find a way to create similar music. He cut eleven more pieces of bamboo of various thicknesses and put them all together to make a twelve-pipe instrument. With it, he was able to catch the range of the phoenix song and make music similar to its tune.

Author's note:

The story of Ma Liang and his magic paintbrush is a popular Chinese folktale which depicts the evil of greed and the honor in helping poor people. It also shows the importance of honing your talents and using your gifts to serve others. There are many myths which depict "culture bearers," or people who contributed to creating culturally beneficial things, like Ling Lun creating the twelve-pipe instrument. Music was, and still is, highly respected in China. It was common for early Taoist scholars to study an instrument and master it as part of their learning.

Chapter 3 – Natural Disasters

The Archer Yi

The Archer

In its infancy, the earth had ten suns. Fortunately, the suns all rotated and took turns shining their light on earth, and all was well. The elder brother always started these cycles and was then followed by the rest of his siblings, each one taking his turn, before the last one finally gave way to the moon, allowing the earth to rest.

One day, the second sun decided it wanted to start shining first. Always it had been the eldest sun—why should it be so? Were they not all bright shining suns? So, the second sun joined the first and shone its light on earth. The other siblings agreed and joined in too. Suddenly, ten suns were radiating all their glory towards the earth and the earth began to suffer.

Where once trees and fields had grown, now they were all dried up. Explosions began to happen as things caught fire left and right. Very quickly, the earth was becoming a volcano, constantly ablaze, and would soon die. There was famine across the land and people were dropping dead like flies.

Yi, an archer and hunter, saw how life and nature was dying all around him and he was outraged. He grabbed his bow and the best arrows he had and headed to the tallest of mountains. After a long climb, he finally reached the top. He felt the searing heat of the tens suns incessantly shining, since the moon no longer arrived with her cool embrace. He was greeted by a god who handed him a vermilion bow and arrows with silk cords. Notching one the arrows on his new bow, Yi fired it. The arrow flew true and struck one of the suns. Instantly its light was snuffed out and it fell from the sky like a great phoenix, but never to be reborn. Yi continued, shooting down suns, until only one was left and finally balance was restored to earth. The last sun promised to only shine in its cycle and to always give way to the moon.

Reward

As thanks for his service towards mankind and earth, Yi was given an elixir of immortality. Yi took the elixir, as it would be rude to refuse, but did not consume it. He knew that if he did he would one day have to watch his wife, Chang'e, die and continue to live without her for eternity. They both agreed that they would store the elixir safely in their house but not drink it, for neither wanted to be without the other.

Yi had an apprentice named Feng Meng, who was without a doubt the second-best archer in the world, surpassed only by his master. Feng Meng realized that the only way he could be the best was to kill his master—or become immortal.

One day when Yi was out hunting monsters who had been preying on the nearby villages, Feng Meng feigned sickness and instead went to Yi's house. Feng Meng broke his way into Yi's house and searched for the elixir. When he finally entered the bedroom, he saw Chang'e with tears running down her face. In her hands was the elixir of immortality.

"Why do you do this to your master? He has trained you since you were a boy!" she said, looking at him.

"I cannot live in his shadow forever. This is the only way to surpass him," Feng Meng said, his mind set. He notched an arrow and pulled it back to his cheek. "Give me the elixir."

Chang'e looked at him sadly and tipped the bottle. Feng Meng lunged for it, not realizing it was already empty.

"As soon as I heard you sneak in, I drank it. I would rather suffer eternally than let the world suffer forever at the hand of a traitor like you." With her last words, she flew to the sky and disappeared to the moon, where she could always watch over her husband. Some of the gods were upset that she had drank the elixir as it had been meant for Yi, but they decided to give her the moon as her residence since her final act as a mortal had also been one of bravery.

When Yi finally returned home and learned what had happened, he fell to his knees and wept. Eventually he found the strength to rise and gathered all of Chang'e's favorite fruits and cakes and sacrificed them to her. The villagers who lived nearby were grateful for his heroic deeds and sympathetic to his cause, so they too sacrificed cakes to the moon. Thus, on every August 15 in the lunar calendar, people eat moon cakes to remember Yi and his beloved wife.

Feng Meng had not given up his hope of being the best. He knew he was still no match for Yi in an archery competition and couldn't become the best using any fair method. Instead he lay in wait, biding his time for Yi to come to the nearby forest. Once Yi passed by, Feng Meng struck him with a club made from a peach tree and killed him. However, Yi's fame was already secured and he became an icon and was worshipped by some as the god who diverts disasters.

Shen Nong – The First Farmer

Once upon a time, there was a man named Shen Nong. Shen Nong saw all the vast varieties of plants and trees that surrounded him, each with their own fruits and leaves. He quickly tried a few of them and realized they tasted differently. Some gave energy and were good to cook, while others were bitter or sour. He began to classify and organize them all, teaching others about which herbs or fruits were good to eat, which had healing properties, and which were poisonous. Many times, he would find a new plant, try it, and end up sick for days because of its toxic nature. However, none of this stopped him from exploring all of China and noting down the properties of all of the herbs and plants. Whenever Shen Nong found plants that were good for eating or healing, he would take them home and plant them on his farm. So, not only did Shen Nong establish the traditional Chinese healing arts, he also created the practice of agriculture. While he was farming, he realized he needed a tool to work the land and invented the plow. All the others who had started farming were soon also using the plow, which Shen Nong gladly taught them how to make and use.

One day, Shen Nong found a new plant that he had never seen before and immediately tasted it. The toxins spread through his body and he became deathly ill. Shen Nong was put in his bed and everyone knew he would soon die. Heaven looked down and saw all that Shen Nong had done for the people, how he had classified and tried all sorts of herbs and plants to help people and how he had made the plow to help the farmers. They granted him immortality. He instantly became well and continued to help people and try plants for many years before he went up to Heaven.

Taming the Rivers

In the dawn of China, the rivers ran rampant in the land, and there were many floods where people and houses were destroyed. Heaven cared not, as it believed the humans deserved it; indeed, they encouraged it. One god, Gun, who was the grandchild to the Jade Emperor, felt differently. Gun felt compassion for the humans and went down to help them. He walked along the river and started to build canals and dig ditches to lead the rivers in ways that would be beneficial to the land and the people. Gun knew the farmers already worked hard and tried to make the rivers aid them rather than hinder them.

When the other gods saw what he was doing, they were upset and smote him down. They stripped him of his immortality and killed him. However, out of his body a dragon was born. It was large, like a river, and was called Yu. The dragon saw the destruction that the rivers were still causing and flew all the way up to heaven to plead on behalf of the humans. When the ruler of heaven finally heard of the vast atrocities and realized the impact that the floods were having on the people, he finally relented and allowed Yu to get to work to ease their suffering. Heaven had also seen how hard the people were working to appease the rivers and appreciated their valiant effort. The dragon Yu raised mountains and redirected rivers to help the land and the people. He also told the people where to build canals that would allow the excess water of the river to flow out in safe ways. Through Yu and the hard work of the people, the floods ceased and the rivers were tamed.

Author's note:

There are numerous legends and myths surrounding the archer Yi—in some he is a hero, in others a villain, in some an immortal, and in other cases a human. The story that follows is a fusion of a few of these that will give you a small glimpse into his vast fame.

Shen Nong literally means "god of agriculture"; he was also very popular among botanists and physicians and often worshipped by them.

Rivers were vital to China's prosperity and were often thought to be huge, wild dragons raging in force. There are numerous myths of how the rivers were subdued and finally brought to aid the people. The archer Yi faces a river in some myths and so does the Monkey King. Historically speaking, China managed to build great ditches and dams with its vast amount of people and workforce to tame the rivers.

Chapter 4 – Li Tieguai – A Taoist Myth

Li Tieguai was a solitary man. He had withdrawn from the village life to live in a secluded cave. The busyness of village life was not for him, nor did he find the gossip appealing. Instead, he became self-sustainable and grew enough vegetables to provide for his simple meals. There was a forest nearby where he cut his own wood to make small fires and keep his mountain cave warm. The mountain also had a small stream, from which he got his water. Alongside the mountain, he had a few terraces where he grew his rice. Li Tieguai felt he had everything he needed. Each day was the same—he would work his land and then withdraw in the evening to read his Taoist scriptures. If the weather was fierce and stormy, he would spend the whole day with his scrolls.

One day as he was planting his seeds, a woodcutter appeared. Li Tieguai had never seen him before but offered him some rice and tea. The stranger talked and talked, mostly about strange things, like spirits, ghosts, and magicians. Li Tieguai listened patiently to everything.

"You are destined for great things," the stranger said. "You will be recognized as a man of wisdom and compassion and you will comfort those in need. One day, you will even be made immortal in recognition of your service."

"Wisdom is a difficult path and few can follow it—how can I ever hope to attain it? I have never pursued immortality, but I do study the Tao and I am willing to study hard."

The stranger seemed happy with Li Tieguai's response and dropped the topic. Instead, he asked, "My wisdom lacks in the ways of nature and spirits, even though I have heard many stories. I have a daughter who desires to honor me and wants me to have a long and healthy life. To do this, she wishes to study so that she can bless me in the best way. She needs a wise teacher. Will you teach her?"

Li Tieguai shook his head. "How can I do that when I myself have so much to learn?"

The stranger nodded. "You could be right." Then he left.

Three days later, the woodcutter was back. This time a beautiful girl was with him.

"This is my only daughter," the woodcutter said. "Ever since I told her of you, she has wanted nothing but to be your student. She has even stopped eating. I have had no choice but to bring her to you. Please be her teacher."

Li Tieguai looked away from the girl and back at his cave, but it was too late. The woodcutter had already disappeared with a quick remark for the girl to obey Li Tieguai in everything.

The girl approached him and knelt at his feet. Li Tieguai flushed and went back to the cave. He sat down in his corner and picked up his Taoist scriptures to study. The fire shone its light for him and kept him warm. The girl had followed him inside and started to prepare dinner for them. While it was cooking, she even cleaned the cave.

After a while, Li Tieguai felt her looking at him again.

"Master," she said. "I do not wish to disturb you in your studies. I know they are important to you. But surely you need company too. Do you not want a wife and a family to care for you when you are old?"

Li Tieguai continued to read, ignoring her.

"Please tell me your thoughts, great master. It is only the two of us here. I will not share your secrets or your doubts. You can talk to me."

He said nothing and walked to the entrance of the cave and stared outside.

"Master, I have to confess something. I did not come here to be a student, but I needed to escape my father. He had planned for me to marry an ugly man with enormous ears who walks with a limp. His whole body is twisted and hairy, unlike yours. You are a handsome man and I would love to be your wife and study with you."

Li Tieguai kept his silence and the girl continued, "I would be the best housewife you could imagine. You would want for nothing."

She kept telling him how good their life together could be as he silently stood there. Many hours passed and she even drew a picture of what their family life could look like. Finally, the night air grew cold and it was bedtime.

Li Tieguai waited until he could finally hear a steady rhythm in the girl's breathing, ensuring that she was asleep. He pulled his mattress to the corner of the cave far away from the girl and then fell asleep.

Rain poured down outside and thunder roared, startling the girl awake. She spotted Li Tieguai in his corner and snuck close to him, cuddling up beside him. Suddenly, Li Tieguai was awake and could feel the warm body of the girl next to him.

"What are you doing?" he asked, worried. "Go away, leave me."

But she only snuggled in closer, shivering. She was wearing nothing but a thin cotton dress.

"Hug me and hold me close. I'm so cold. I need your warmth."

Li Tieguai rolled further and further into the corner of the cave, growing colder as he did so. The girl kept following, whispering gently, even asking him to take her as his wife. Li Tieguai blushed again, but kept his eyes shut and tried to forget about the girl. This continued throughout the night, but Li Tieguai remained strong.

When dawn finally came, the woodcutter was back. Li Tieguai was washing his pots and had not seen the girl anywhere since last night.

"Where is my daughter?" the man asked.

"I don't know. She suddenly vanished last night."

"What did you do? Did you hurt her? Did you rape her? Why would she just vanish? What have you done?"

Li Tieguai held up his hands and shook his head. "I would never do such a thing. I have not touched your daughter nor harmed her."

The woodcutter smiled. "I know," he said. "You are a man of firm conviction and a man of honor. You have a deep understanding of Taoism and you are committed to the pursuit of it. We are similar, you and I."

Suddenly, the woodcutter transformed and became a bearded man in a long blue robe. It was Lao Zi, the immortal founder of Taoism.

"I sent the girl to tempt you and test you. You have shown true integrity and that you are not easily tricked."

Lao Zi brought out a small dumpling from his robe and gave it to Li Tieguai.

"Swallow it," he said.

Li Tieguai did as he was instructed and felt a surge of energy within him that never ceased. From then on, he was never tired, ill, thirsty, or even hungry. He began to travel the land, helping the poor and needy by defending their causes. Every few months, he would return to his cave to meditate and study the Taoist scriptures.

Li Tieguai Tempted by Treasure

Another day when Li Tieguai had been back in the cave to meditate and study his books, he took a break to study the forest. While he was walking and observing, he noticed two men. They looked nervous and secretive and were glancing around to make sure no one was looking. Li Tieguai kept himself hidden behind a tree and watched. The men had two big woven sacks and they looked heavy and full to the brim. The men searched in the tree and dug out a small alcove and stuffed the bags into it. They looked around again and, seeing no one, left the area.

Li Tieguai decided to leave too. He came back daily and noticed that the bags were still hidden. It seemed like stolen goods, but he had no idea who it had been taken from.

He went down to the village but heard nothing of anything missing. Instead, he met an old man who asked to drink tea with him. Li Tieguai, being polite, readily accepted and they sat and dined together.

"I can see that you will be a very wealthy man," the stranger said.

"You could be right," Li Tieguai responded. "I know where two bags of gold are hidden." Li Tieguai told the old man of what he had seen in the forest.

"You should take it," the man said. "It is stolen anyway. Without money you will end up bitter and unhappy. Why not go now and make sure you get the money? You can even use it to help people."

Li Tieguai shrugged off the old man's urging. "I have no need for it. I am happy with what I have."

"Your fortunes could change. A little insurance never goes amiss."

But Li Tieguai held firm. He could help people with what he had; stolen goods were not the way to earn money. Possessions were meaningless and he was content. He parted ways with the old man.

A few days later, they met again. But this time, the man's attitude had changed.

"Here, eat this," he said, holding out a dumpling for him. Li Tieguai felt he could trust the old man and did as he was told.

Immediately, he began to feel lighter as if he could float.

The man transformed before him and was now wearing long blue robes. It was Lao Zi who had come to test him again.

When Li Tieguai began to walk away, he realized he was moving much faster than before. As he walked through the town and past the temple, he was traveling faster than a swallow. Soon, he was traveling so fast that his body lifted and he soared into the air. He could fly and could now reach even more villages with his aid and counsel than before.

Li Tieguai Takes an Apprentice

Li Tieguai was now respected as a learned man and continued to help the poor and spread Taoist teachings. With his speed and flight, along with never being ill or tired, his fame had spread quickly. Eventually, Li Tieguai took on an apprentice named Li Qing. This had been at Lao Zi's request and Li Tieguai had become an official disciple of him.

One day, he was called to meet with Lao Zi again at a mountain far away.

"I must leave you," Li Tieguai said to his apprentice. "I have been summoned and must travel to Penglai Mountain.

"But that is thousands of miles away!" his student exclaimed. "It will take months to get there."

"Do not question me," Li Tieguai responded. "I will leave my body here and my soul will travel to converse with Lao Zi. If I am not back within seven days, you can burn my body, for I will have become immortal. If you study hard enough and live a life of servitude, perhaps one day you can become immortal too."

Li Tieguai then sat down and began to meditate. After a while, Li Qing saw a shimmer of smoke leave Li Tieguai's body. He put his hand in front of his master's nose and felt no breath. Being a sincere and loyal student, Li Qing did not leave his master's body for six days. However, on the morning of the seventh day, a messenger arrived.

"You must come with me," the messenger said. "Your mother is gravely ill and wants to see you before she dies."

The disciple knew it was the seventh day, so with a heavy heart, he burned his master's body and went with the messenger to see his dying mother.

On the way to his mother, not far from the cave, he met a beggar dying by the roadside. He knelt by the man to see what he could do to help and soon saw that the man was already beyond saving; there was nothing he could do. The man had short hair, ragged clothes, long eyebrows, and a disfigured leg. Next to him lay a wooden crutch, thrown to the side.

That same evening, Li Tieguai's spirit came back to look for his body. But it was nowhere to be found. He searched and searched and could not even find his disciple. Li Tieguai realized it was the seventh day and then saw the fire and the burnt ashes next to it. His body was gone. He needed to find a body fast or else he would no longer be immortal. Looking around, Li Tieguai found the deformed beggar's body that his disciple had seen earlier in the day. He knew he had no other choice and reluctantly entered the body. Just as he fit into his new form, he heard someone laugh behind him. There stood an old man with a bag of herbs and potions.

"What is so funny?" asked Li Tieguai. "Do you know me?"

"I do indeed know you. Here, take this potion. It will heal the wounds of your body and restore your health."

Li Tieguai received the potion and drank it. Immediately the vial refilled.

"This potion will never stop. With it you have the gift of healing and will be of great comfort to many people. Everyone, rich or poor, will want you to visit their home, regardless of your unfortunate looks." The old man picked up the wooden crutch next to Li Tieguai.

"This crutch shall be your aid and never falter, never rust, and never fail you." As the man spoke, the crutch changed and became iron. "From this day on, you shall join the immortals, but now I must return to Lao Zi, as I am merely his messenger."

With that, the old man started walking away down the path. But as he walked he transformed and Li Tieguai knew he had met Lao Zi again.

Li Tieguai walked the land, supported by his staff. Now he was immortal and he never ceased helping the sick and the poor.

Author's note:

Taoist mythology has a total of eight immortals of which Li Tieguai is one. His name (tie guai) actually means "iron crutch" as he was known for having a deformed leg and always walked around with his iron crutch to support himself. He is meant to have been quite ugly and perhaps the story you just read is a way of explaining why that was. But even above that, it showed that looks do not matter – what matters is helping others and seeking knowledge.

Taoists strived for knowledge and immortality and their myths show this too. Seeking immortality is the height of knowledge and the noblest thing you can do, according to Taoism.

Chapter 5 – Sun Wukong – The Monkey King

The Monkey King's Birth

In the red mountains, on top of the highest of peaks, stood a strange rock. It balanced on the edge of the mountaintop as if it would fall over at any second. For generations it had stood there, until one day, during a furious lightning storm, a lightning bolt cracked the rock open and out came a monkey. In many ways he was not like a monkey at all. He was brilliant, clever, cunning, and mischievous. But he was also faster, stronger, taller and more agile than any other monkey ever seen before.

The monkey stretched, finally awakening to life. Coming down the mountain, he found kinsmen— other monkeys—and they set out to find a home. They found a lush, beautiful mountain full of fruit and flowers. There they lived and basked in the bounties of the mountain. For a while, the monkey was happy there. The other monkeys had soon realized that he was more capable than any of them and named him king of their tribe and even of all monkeys in the world. He was now known as the Monkey King. However, eventually the Monkey King began to grow restless. Despite all the food and the good life that he lived, he realized he was still mortal and would one day die. This frustrated him and he knew he had to pursue the noblest of things—immortality. He left the mountain of fruit and flowers and found a Taoist master.

As the Taoist master's disciple, the Monkey King soon became his best student. He learned how to fly, how to clone himself and become a mirage, and he even mastered the 72 transformations, which allowed him to turn into anything he wanted. The Taoist master was so impressed with the Monkey King's talents that he renamed him Sun Wukong, meaning "Awakened to Emptiness."

Finding a Weapon

Sun Wukong was pleased with all the skills that he had picked up, but knew that he was still a mortal and that his days were numbered. He decided that he needed a weapon and armor worthy of all his skills and talent. Leaving the Taoist master, he met an old monkey who told him of the Dragon King, Ao Guang. Ao Guang's palace had thousands of weapons and he had supplied most of Heaven with their arsenal of weapons. There, the Monkey King should find a weapon worthy of his skill.

Sun Wukong flew to the Eastern Sea where he swam below the surface and looked for the palace. Eventually, at the bottom of the sea, he found a huge palace, guarded by crustaceans dressed in armor and armed with halberds and swords. Even without a weapon, Sun Wukong found them to be no match to his skills and soon entered the palace. One of the guards tried to run and warn the Dragon King of this intruder, but it was too late, as Sun Wukong was already there in the throne room.

"What is this monkey doing in my palace without an invitation? Guards! Take him away!" Ao Guang shouted, outraged at the insolence and lack of respect of Sun Wukong.

Sun Wukong merely laughed and jumped out of the way of the guards. He toyed with them, first disappearing into thin air, before reappearing and disarming them.

The Dragon King looked at Sun Wukong with new respect, but also fear. He had no desire to let a monkey destroy his palace.

"What do you want? Why do you disturb me?" The Dragon King's voice was angry and annoyed, but there was a touch of respect in it too.

"I need a weapon. As you can see, I am skilled and able, but I lack a weapon that is worthy of me. I hear you make good weapons. Give me one and I will leave you in peace."

The Dragon King fixed his eyes on the audacious monkey, and then quickly gestured to the still dazed guards and servants. "Fetch him a few weapons to try."

They scurried away and soon came back with an array of weapons.

First, a spear was brought to Sun Wukong. The guard was barely able to lift it, such was its weight. Sun Wukong spun it around as if it was a chopstick and then dropped it to the floor. "Far too flimsy," he said. The guard looked at him with new awe as he struggled to retrieve the spear.

Next came a giant sword. It was carried by several guards and the Dragon King was near certain that this would be far too heavy for the monkey.

Sun Wukong looked at the sword with his mouth agape and walked around it as if contemplating how he would pick it up. But there was a glint of mischief in his eyes and suddenly he stopped his charade and took up the sword, swishing it in the air before twirling it around on the palm of his hand.

Now the Dragon King trembled. "Bring him the heaviest weapon we have," he ordered.

Finally, out came a massive halberd carried by dozens of guards. Sun Wukong approached it and tried to pick it up. Seeing the monkey struggle made the Dragon King smile, but just as he did, Sun Wukong burst into laughter and threw the mighty weapon into the air as if it was a feather. "This is truly the heaviest you have? It feels like a comb. Don't you have anything heavier?"

Now the Dragon King was truly desperate. He needed to be rid of this monkey. He couldn't stand being ridiculed anymore. Just then his wife swam into the hall and whispered in his ear, "There's a pillar that's been glowing for the past few days, perhaps it is fated to be the monkey's."

Together, they all swam to see this pillar. It was located deep in the palace in a courtyard. Sun Wukong's eyes lit with real joy when he saw it. The pillar was massive and towered upwards beyond what they could see. It was wide, and even hugging it, Sun Wukong could not grasp his arms fully around it.

The Dragon King started to whisper to his wife. "Will anything happen if he actually does manage to take it? The pillar is there for the stability of the sea."

"It's mostly symbolic," she said.

Just then, Sun Wukong lifted the pillar up and swung it around, but his movements were awkward and barely controlled. The royal couple had to quickly dodge and swim to the side to avoid getting struck.

"Perhaps it should be a little smaller," Sun Wukong muttered to himself. Immediately, the pillar shrank to the size of a long fighting stick. The Monkey King laughed with delight. This truly was the weapon for him. He rapidly spun and twirled it around, trying out his moves. The weapon moved with such fury that huge water currents formed and nearly swept away the entire court.

Sun Wukong laughed again and then changed the pole's shape. First it became big, then small, then medium, before he finally made it as small as a needle and tucked it behind his ear, ready for any future battle.

Upsetting Heaven

Armed with his new weapon and shiny golden, impenetrable armor (a gift from the Dragon King to ensure the monkey would leave), Sun Wukong explored the world in search for immortality and because he wanted to show the world what he could do. First, he encountered demons and immortals and overwhelmed them all, either through force or simple mischief and nuisance. Eventually, the king of the underworld heard of him and decided to capture him. He managed to kidnap the monkey while he was sleeping but regretted his action as soon as Sun Wukong woke up.

Seeing that he was in the underworld, Sun Wukong decided to make the best of it. With his pole always in his hand, he fought his way free from all of the guards and then started to look for the book of the judge, the book that the king of the underworld owned. Unmatched in speed and illusion, Sun Wukong eventually found the book deep in the underworld. Turning the pages, he finally saw his own name. Written after it were the words, *Dies at the age of 342*. He quickly erased his name, thinking that this should ensure his immortality. He left the underworld, happy knowing that he had finally obtained immortality.

This action upset all of the other immortals, of course. Never before had anyone simply struck out their name from the book to become eternal. Immortality was something earned, something given to those that had achieved greatness or who had learned the most important lessons in life. The king of the underworld complained that his dominion had been defiled and that the Monkey King had robbed him of one of his powers.

The Jade Emperor was also upset and decided to take action. He had heard of the monkey's exploits and knew that direct confrontation should be a last resort. Instead, he invited the Monkey King up to Heaven to join the imperial palace as the Protector of the Horses of the Imperial Stables. At first, Sun Wukong was excited and happy to finally be recognized by the gods. Finally, he was getting what he and his skills deserved. However, after only a few days at his new job, he realized that the Jade Emperor was simply giving him a task to keep him occupied and out of mischief. He had become nothing more than a horse groom.

Sun Wukong was furious and decided to revolt. Heaven's warriors were sent out to fight him but proved to be no match. Sun Wukong stood firm, unscathed, and surrounded by disarmed and embarrassed warriors. He proclaimed himself to be the Great Sage Equal to Heaven. Now all the immortals of Heaven were angry with him, the Jade Emperor most of all. Seeing that his warriors were no match for the Monkey King, the Jade Emperor tried to calm and appease Sun Wukong with a new title and gave him the honor of guarding the peach orchards. Sun Wukong accepted this and calmed down, but still continued to call himself the Great Sage Equal to Heaven.

One day, the Queen-Empress was having a banquet with all the deities, but the Great Sage Equal to Heaven was not on the list to be invited. Sun Wukong soon found out and was yet again furious. He started his tantrum by eating all the peaches in the peach orchard, which are not regular peaches, but peaches of immortality, giving himself immortality a second time. This was not enough for him. Knowing that everyone was at the party, the Monkey King sneaked into Laozi's quarter, the great Taoist founder himself, and stole a few of his pills of immortality. Having ensured his immortality thrice over, he felt ready to challenge Heaven. He crashed the party turning over tables, drinking the imperial wine, and challenging all who dared to oppose him. A few of the deities tried to take control and fight him, but to no avail. The Jade Emperor ordered 100,000 warriors to take him down. Alone, Sun Wukong still won, his pole becoming every size it needed to take his opponents down.

The great deities then saw what the Monkey King had done to the orchard, and Laozi realized that his house has been plundered. Laozi and the three-eyed Er Lang Shen joined forces with the rest of Heaven and managed to subdue and capture the monkey at last. They tried to kill him with fire, axes, and poison, but nothing worked. Sun Wukong was unkillable and a true immortal. Laozi then threw Sun Wukong into the Eight Trigram Furnace, hoping that would kill him. But even after 49 days of the most excruciating fires, searing flames, and alchemy of the Taoist scholars, the monkey remained alive. He was sizzling, but unscathed and still as dangerous. In fact, he was even more dangerous, as the fires had given him incredible vision that could penetrate and see through anything. Sun Wukong burst free and challenged the gods once again, daring anyone to face him.

Heaven was desperate, as none of the gods could best the Monkey King. The Jade Emperor pleaded with the Buddha, the greatest being in the universe, to help them. The Buddha came and talked to Sun Wukong, holding him in his palm.

"Why do you wish to rule over Heaven?" the Buddha asked the monkey.

"I am the most powerful creature in the whole universe," he answered. "I can beat any of the deities here in Heaven. I am the strongest and I can jump thousands of miles in only one jump, being anywhere I want to in an instant."

"If you are so strong, then I challenge you to a dare."

The monkey was instantly excited. He excelled at challenges. He was the best. "I accept," Sun Wukong said, without hesitation.

"I want to see if you can jump out of my hand. It should be easy for you. After all, you can jump thousands of miles."

The Monkey King laughed and jumped to the edge of the universe. Five pillars surrounded him and he peed on them to mark that he had been there. Then he jumped back, ready to gloat. But nothing changed. Instead, the pillars became Buddha's five fingers. In fact, he had never left Buddha's hand. Sun Wukong had been defeated and as punishment for all the havoc he had caused, Buddha trapped him under the mountain where he had come from. For five hundred years, the Monkey King was trapped and left to think over all of what he had done.

Sun Wukong - The Buddhist Disciple

Time passed and the Monkey King was kept under the mountain, locked away from the world to ensure that he would cause no mischief.. A Buddhist monk, who had been thrown out of Heaven and was doing penance for his sins, was now in his tenth lifetime. This time he was asked to go on a mission to the west to find sacred Buddhist scriptures and bring them into China. The monk's name was XuanZang, or Tang Seng. China had changed and moved into the Tang dynasty, where the roads were dangerous and things were not as they once were. The monk was frail and unequipped to go alone on this perilous journey. Guan Yin, the Goddess of Mercy, knew this and asked Buddha what they could do. He asked Heaven for the permission to release Sun Wukong to be the monk's protector. Heaven agreed, not able to argue against the Buddha. Besides, the Buddha was not simply going to release the mischievous Monkey King without precautions. He created a magical golden headband that would go on Sun Wukong's head which would allow Tang Seng to control him. If the Monkey King tried to do anything that was not permitted or was displeasing to Tang Seng, he would feel paralyzing pain in his head, utterly disabling him. Buddha and Guan Yin hoped that this journey to the west would teach both Tang Seng and Sun Wukong lessons and help them find the true meaning of being a Buddhist.

As soon as Sun Wukong was set free, he felt the golden headband on his head and tried to remove it, but instantly felt pain that filled his entire being. With the pain searing through him, he was thrown to the ground and unable to move. He submitted to Tang Seng and agreed to join him in the recovery of the texts. Together, they encountered 81 tribulations and trials, fought demons and temptations, and became better beings.

Early in their journey, they met two other characters who joined their cause.

Pigsy (Zhu Bajie)

One of the admirals of heaven, one of many of the deities that Sun Wukong had fought and beaten when he caused havoc in heaven, was flawed to a high degree. Zhu Bajie was in charge of 80,000 sailors, but would often get drunk, eat far too much, and try to seduce and sleep with young maidens and other women; in other words, he was far too easily swayed by all the sins of the flesh. One day, he saw the moon goddess Chang'e pass by. He was already drunk and found her beauty intoxicating. Zhu Bajie advanced towards her, flirted, and tried to force her into sleeping with him. This was the final act that condemned him, and he was instantly banished from Heaven and sent to Earth in the form of a pig with human capabilities. Pigsy, as he was now known due to his form, was huge, fat, and had all the features of a pig, but could walk on two legs, talk, and fight. Everyone shied away from him for he was an abomination and looked monstrous. He made a home for himself in a cave, but ventured into villages for food.

One day, the goddess Guan Yin passed by, looking for people to protect Tang Seng on his journey to find the sacred scriptures. Seeing Pigsy in the cave, she stopped.

"Do you wish for redemption, to atone for your past and become better?" she asked him.

He bowed down on the ground. "Yes, I do. I am repentant," he said.

"A monk and a monkey will pass here soon. You will become a monk and join them as their companion."

"Yes, goddess," he said.

With that, Guan Yin disappeared.

A few months later, Sun Wukong and Tang Seng passed by a village near Pigsy's cave. There they saw a monstrous pig-like being dragging a young girl. "I will marry you," he shouted, as the girl cried, struggling against the big pig-beast. Tang Seng quickly gave his assent to allow Sun Wukong to intervene. The Monkey King somersaulted next to the pig and hit him hard in the chest. Pigsy dropped the girl, furious at the intervention. He roared and tried to ram the monkey, but Sun Wukong laughed and jumped into the air, appearing behind the pig and kicking him hard on his backside. Pigsy squealed in pain and became red in his face. He tried to fight again, but now Sun Wukong had lost his patience. He took out his fighting pole, made it large, and swept Pigsy onto his back. Then he leaped close, pinning him down.

"What do we do with people who cannot control their lust?" he asked Tang Seng the monk.

"We teach them control," the monk answered. "Let him go."

Sun Wukong did as he was told, fearing the pain of the golden headband, but he kept a careful eye on Pigsy who was still scarlet in his face. He bowed to the monk and finally to the monkey. Just then, Guan Yin appeared again.

"This is your other companion," she told Tang Seng. Sun Wukong stared at her in astonishment, insulted that his protection was not enough and that this pig was to now join them.

Tang Seng merely bowed his head at her, ever tranquil. And so, they became three and they set out on their journey to the west.

Sandy (Sha Wujing)

Not long after Pigsy joined Tang Seng and Sun Wukong, they came to a long, massive river. Not only was it impassable, it was also guarded by a terrible, fierce beast who feasted on any humans who strayed too close. But this was the path that the companions had to take on their pilgrimage and they needed the monster to be able to cross the river, as no one else would be able to bring them across.

As Pigsy and Tang Seng approached the river, the massive fish monster leaped out of the water and became an ogre. He had red, matted hair, a long magical staff in his hand, and a necklace of nine skulls around his neck. He attacked and Pigsy tried to fight him. For a while they were locked in combat, each trying to strike each other and both able to deflect each other too well. Even when a hit actually landed, neither seemed to care, but continued fighting. Sun Wukong, whose sight allowed him to see the work of demons and witches, was away fighting a demon, but when he finally appeared, the ogre immediately turned into a fish and jumped back into the river. Even this fish-ogre had heard of Sun Wukong and knew he would meet his match.

However, as soon as the Monkey King disappeared on another mission, the ogre returned and began to fight Pigsy yet again. It became clear that Pigsy could not defeat him, but neither could the monster defeat Pigsy. Sun Wukong appeared and again the ogre instantly jumped back into the river as a great fish. This time though, Sun Wukong created a copy of himself and pretended to leave, while he waited for the ogre to show up again. As soon as the ogre reappeared on land, Sun Wukong fought him and forced him into submission.

Again, Guan Yin appeared.

"This is Sandy and he shall be your fourth and final companion. Together you will all make the journey to find the sacred scriptures," she said, before turning to the ogre. "You shall redeem yourself in this quest. Your punishment will no longer pursue you here on Earth as long as you devote yourself to this pilgrimage and complete it."

He bowed and thanked her. With that, she disappeared.

"What did you do?" Pigsy asked.

"Once, I was a general in Heaven. But one day, I accidentally knocked over the Queen Empress' goblet, shattering it. With that, I lost my title and was banished to Earth in this grotesque form." As he said that, he gained his human features back, his red hair changing into black. He laughed happily. "I am grateful for this quest of yours and this opportunity."

"She mentioned a punishment that pursued you?" the Monkey King asked, gazing intently at him.

"I live in a river to hide. Before being thrown out, I was whipped 800 times and then cursed. Every day here on Earth swords would come down and stab me, but they cannot reach me in the river. It was my one refuge."

The Monkey King nodded, but there was clear anger in his eyes. Then he put his hands to his temples, rubbing them as if a faint buzz of pain had whispered to him for even thinking that the gods were unjust.

"Please, now that you are with us, help us cross the river," Tang Seng said.

Sandy brought forth a gourd, which he turned into a boat for them to cross in and so they continued on their pilgrimage for the sacred texts.

Author's Note:

The legend of the Monkey King is well-known and perhaps the most famous of all of China's legends, which is why it has been given a bit more space in this book. It shows the clear multi-layers of thought and beliefs that exist in Chinese mythology. At first, we see that the Monkey King is a devout Taoist student. That said, he does not really help people with his skills, which is a failure in that belief, but he does master himself and his body and ultimately achieves immortality—the greatest possible achievement for any Taoist. We are meant to read him as being too arrogant and chaotic in the Chinese literary classic *The Journey to the West*, where Sun Wukong must learn to control himself and serve the Buddhistic purpose. It is also from this book and this movement towards Buddhism within China and Chinese thought that Buddha is emphasized as the ultimate being, even above the Jade Emperor and Laozi. However, even within this Chinese Buddhistic text, we still see all the elements of old Chinese mythology—there are demons and deities and most of the companions and even enemies have been brought in from other tales of old and then remade into this narrative.

Sun Wukong is easy to love because he is incredibly talented and brilliant but also mischievous and unpredictable. He has been drafted into computer games, modern animated series, and movies and will most likely continue to be a cultural icon in China.

Chapter 6 – The Investiture of the Gods

King Zhou's Hubris

During the Shang dynasty, around 1100 BC, the kings were harsher and crueler. One king was called Da Yi, and he had three sons. One day, he was walking in the garden and admiring its beauty. Suddenly, a corner of the pavilion fell. Thankfully, his youngest son, Prince Zhou, was there to catch it, supporting it with his bare hands. The ministers and advisers were all impressed and told the king to make his youngest son the next king, as he would have the strength to rule the kingdom.

However, physical strength is not enough to run a kingdom and when Zhou became king he showed that he was also cruel and foolhardy. He waged war and was successful, but his ministers started to warn him that his successes would soon cease unless he paid homage to the gods. King Zhou followed the advice he was given and went to the temple of Nüwa. He placed his incense by the altar and murmured a quick prayer. Suddenly, a draft blew through the temple and the great curtain that veiled the depiction of the goddess was swept away. Her form, which was never meant to be seen by mere mortals, was revealed. The illustration of her was a masterful piece, portraying her as the woman of all women, as femininity itself. King Zhou was instantly smitten and filled with lust for her. He gaped and stared in awe at her.

"Oh Nüwa, most glorious and beautiful of all women. I hunger for you and need you by my side. If only you were made of flesh, I would marry you this instant."

He kept staring and would not avert his eyes. His ministers and guards were all horrified but dared not lift their eyes in case they too would see Nüwa and dishonor her.

The king broke the silence again and turned to his men: "Quick, get me brushes and ink. I must write a poem to her so she may hear me and meet with me."

His servants could not but obey and soon he was brought the ink he required. King Zhou began to write on the walls of the temple.

Her beauty unmatched, even as fashions of clay and paint,

Forms and figures to make any man want for her,

Fruits which are ripe and firm, with a garden most lush.

Would she only be in flesh, I would have her in my palace.

The ministers were horrified both by the writing now on the wall and by its contents. One of them spoke out:

"My king, I am but your humble servant, but please, Nüwa has always protected our people. She is a goddess and far above our humble station. This poem is an affront. She will not view it lightly and ill will fall upon our kingdom."

"Nonsense," the king said, still full of lust, but with a hint of underlying anger. "This poem is praise to her beauty and all should see it. It is my gift to her and the kingdom. I will hear no more of it."

After that, no one dared to speak, but all trembled in fear of what was to come.

Nüwa's Rage

When Nüwa came back from her trip and arrived at her temple, she saw the blasphemous poem and screamed with rage. She immediately flew down to the palace to kill King Zhou on the spot for his arrogance and dishonor. However, as soon as she saw him, she could see the tendrils of time around him – she saw his fortune, his future and his past. He was to reign twenty-eight more years, as had been decided by Heaven long ago when his ancestor won centuries of luck. She stopped her wrath and knew she would find her revenge through other means.

She summoned three spirits to her temple and sent them forth to bring harm and downfall to King Zhou, but they were to hurt no one else. Should they succeed, she would give them human bodies and life.

Meanwhile, in the palace, King Zhou could think of nothing but Nüwa's beauty. It consumed him day and night. He dreamt of her and thought of her and his kingdom suffered. Ministers that he had always listened to now seemed foolish to him and he begun to appreciate the flattery of fools more. When two of these ministers of flattery came to him, he shared his struggle with them.

"Nothing has purpose or meaning anymore. Nothing compares to Nüwa's beauty. What can I do?" he asked.

"My king," they said. "You must send out a message to all your dukes and ministers. Ask them for the most beautiful girls in the land. With a thousand young maidens to choose a concubine from, you will no longer be lusting over any other beauty."

Their advice made sense to the king and he asked for the decree to go out.

Many of the dukes and ministers were outraged. The king already had a wife and two concubines along with a thousand beautiful women that served him. Surely, he had no need for anymore. All of them knew how much this would upset the people. One of them spoke up and convinced the king to take back his decree. Trusting the minister, who had served his father very well, King Zhou finally agreed to withdraw the decree.

A few years later, it was time for all the dukes and ministers to visit and give gifts. One of them was a straightforward and honest man who did not like the flattering ministers that held the king's ear. These ministers did not like him either and they told the king that this duke, Su Hu, had a most beautiful daughter and taking her as his concubine would not upset the people, as it would be only one woman rather than a thousand. The king liked the idea and sent the message to Su Hu to bring his daughter, as he wanted to see her famed beauty. Su Hu refused and war ensued, but after a few battles, Su Hu gave in and brought himself and his daughter to the palace. On the way there, they were attacked by a vixen spirit, one of the three spirits that had been sent by Nüwa, who killed Su Hu's daughter and took her place.

When they came to the palace, the king was furious to see Su Hu still alive and wanted him executed.

"He has brought his daughter; she is just outside." The king's other ministers advised. "See if she pleases the king's eye first, and if so, pardon Su Hu as he was always a good, loyal duke prior to this incident."

The king agreed and as his eyes fell on Daji, the fox spirit, he fell deeply in love. She was fairer than the fairest summer's eve. Her movements were graceful and she swayed like a cherry blossom in the breeze. He was filled with blind lust for her and instantly pardoned Su Hu. Then he took Daji into his arms, locked eyes with her, and was mesmerized. He asked for the servants to take her to his palace. After they had washed and oiled her, he soon joined her in his palace quarters and they did not leave the room for three months. No one saw the king. Every moment he was awake he spent with Daji, enchanted by her body and looks. The reports were piling in. War had broken out with giants and monsters. Famine had struck the east. But the king stayed in his palace with Daji, indulging in wine and lust, while Nüwa laughed at his decline.

Author's note:

The Investiture of the Gods is a long tale, and this is merely a short extract which shows how it starts. After many battles and many deeds, the tale ends with numerous heroes being exalted into heaven as immortals, thus forming a pantheon of gods, which is how the book got its name. The book is a compilation of myths and legends surrounding this tumultuous time and shows the rise of the Taoist immortals.

Chapter 7 – Three Kingdoms

All things united must eventually divide, and all things divided will eventually unite. The Han dynasty had ruled for a long time, but with the ascension of Emperor Huang, their decline began. He deposed and humiliated many lords, governors, and nobles. Instead, he elevated eunuchs and put them in new positions of power, giving them more and more influence. Other warlords and people were getting angry as corruption spread through the palace and the country. However, nothing happened for a while, and soon Emperor Huang passed away to be replaced by Emperor Ling. Emperor Ling was too young to rule in his own right when he came to power, so Dou Wu, who oversaw the military, and Chen Fan, who oversaw education, ruled in his stead and advised him. They saw the negative influence that the eunuchs had and wanted to end it by plotting the assassination of the chief eunuch. Sadly, it was noticed in time, and instead they were assassinated, which only continued the decline of the Han dynasty.

At this time, crazy incidents began to occur all over the country. Storms were far more frequent, the seas raged in unexpected ways, attacking even the coastal villages in ways they never had before, earthquakes struck towns, and even worse, supernatural incidents took place. The first of these happened to the young emperor himself. He walked into a room to relax and suddenly, with a breeze, a green coiled snake flew in the window and landed on his chair. Emperor Ling was so frightened that he fainted on the spot. His attendants took him away, removing the snake too. In the villages, female hens suddenly turned into male roosters. Rivers flooded, winds blew the wrong directions and there were thunderstorms without any rain. The emperor was terrified and still so young that he did not know what to do. He sent out an edict asking all his advisers what these signs could mean and why they were happening.

One of these advisers was brutally blunt and sent a letter for the emperor's eyes only, blaming it all on the fact that the emperor and the country was ruled by women and eunuchs. However, one of the eunuchs found the letter and read it before it reached the emperor. As soon as the eunuchs read the letter, they began to plot. In no time, they had forced the adviser to be banished and sent to his hometown, removing him from court. After that, the government sunk further into decline and bandits started appearing all over the land as people began to revolt.

At this time, Zhang Jiao, a dissident, met an old man while he was up in the mountains. The man had a long beard and carried a walking stick in one hand and a big tome in the other. This book was called *The Essential Art of Great Peace*, and the man gave it to Zhang Jiao, telling him to study it to achieve peace in the land. The man said he was an immortal sent to give him this book. Zhang Jiao read the book and shared its secrets with his two brothers. The three of them became healers and healed people throughout the land, but it was said that Zhang Jiao could also control weather and much more, as he had become a great sorcerer. Zhang Jiao and his brothers had seen the decline of the kingdom. They decided that the emperor had lost his Mandate of Heaven and that it was time for a new era. This sparked a rebellion which was bloody and gruesome.

Eventually, the emperor's forces vanquished the rebellion under He Jin, the emperor's general. But during this time, Emperor Ling had passed away, possibly assassinated but no one could pinpoint who had been behind it. He Jin placed a new emperor to serve as a figurehead. The eunuchs saw that He Jin was getting far too powerful and did not like this. They feared that soon he would depose them and strip their power, so they had him assassinated. At his death, He Jin's followers rebelled and fought against the eunuchs and their forces. During the commotion, the emperor fled.

Awarlord, Dong Zhuo, found him and took back the imperial city from both He Jin's followers and the eunuchs. He placed the emperor back in power and claimed he had taken the city back for him; but of course, Dong Zhuo held the real power as ruler. He claimed to be protecting the emperor, but soon deposed him and found another child emperor to use as a puppet instead. Dong Zhuo ruled as a tyrant and the land continued to suffer. Attempts were made to assassinate him, but they failed.

One of these assassination attempts was made by a warrior and general called Cao Cao. After his failed effort, he was forced to flee, but he managed to build up a band of followers and warriors. He sent out a fake imperial decree, in which he told all the warlords about Dong Zhuo keeping the emperor as a prisoner and how this tyranny needed to end. The warlords went into alliance with Cao Cao to free the emperor, and together they began to fight back against Dong Zhuo and his persecution. Big battles took place and Cao Cao and his forces won them all, pushing Dong Zhuo back.

Dong Zhuo soon realized that he was fighting a losing battle and retreated from the capital, leaving the emperor there. Instead, he tried to find a stronger defense in his own hometown. Alas, surrounded by family in his own fortress, his son killed him.

Meanwhile, Cao Cao had captured the capital and now had the emperor in his care, who he claimed to protect. In reality, the emperor was still a figurehead, just with a new master puppeteer.

Now, we must travel back in time to visit a young man called Liu Bei. Liu Bei had seen the rebellion take place and the havoc that Zhang Jiao had caused. Liu Bei had always been special and knew that he was sent from heaven. He could trace his lineage many centuries back to Emperor Jing—he was in the line of Heaven's chosen rulers. As Liu Bei saw this rebellion against the imperial family by Zhang Jiao the sorcerer, he was outraged and gathered his own people around him to fight against the uprising. He helped He Jin and the imperial forces to vanquish the rebels, but after the rebellion had been crushed, Liu Bei received hardly any recognition. He was made prefect of a little county, but with the vast amount of corruption present in government, he declined the post.

Liu Bei instead kept fighting; he fought against Dong Zhuo, Dong Zhuo's son, and eventually against Cao Cao.

During the reign of Cao Cao's emperor, the Han kingdom continued its civil war and its decline. In the midst of the chaos, Cao Cao gathered his army to try and reunite China. He battled against Liu Bei and another warlord called Sun Quan, who had been taking territory in the east. Liu Bei and Sun Quan won.

With Cao Cao's death, all pretense of an emperor ruling China was stripped away since his son, Cao Pi, decided to proclaim himself as emperor. Of course, Liu Bei and Sun Quan disagreed, both holding large areas of land in China. They too declared themselves to be kings, and eventually emperors, of their land. Thus, three kingdoms were born and the land was broken in three.

Author's note:

"Three Kingdoms" is multi-faceted. It is a historical period of time where the country was split into three kingdoms, and it is also a work of literature in the form of *The Romance of the Three Kingdoms*, which weaves together orally kept legends, myths, and history.

This story, along with *The Investiture of the Gods*, showcases what it means to lose the Mandate of Heaven, which is an incredibly important concept in China, even today. It means that the ruling authorities are seen to be chosen by Heaven and are meant to rule. However, as soon as the kingdom is in decline and there are signs that show disfavor from Heaven, it means that the Mandate has been broken which in turn allows for rebellion and revolt. This idea is also shown in the Monkey King story; because the Jade Emperor and the Taoist pantheon could not defeat Sun Wukong, their time had passed and this showed the necessity of Buddhism and how it had become the dominant belief at that time.

Chapter 8 – Modern Mythology – The Bottle Gourd Children

Once upon a time, an old man was climbing in the mountains searching for herbs with healing powers. He stumbled upon a mountain that was shaped exactly like a bottle gourd. As he was climbing, he tripped and fell. What he did not know was that in his fall he had freed two evil spirits that had been locked underneath the mountain for a long time. One was female with the body of a snake, while the other was a man with aspects of a scorpion. Both of them had magical powers and immediately began to terrorize the nearby villages as they had done before they had been captured.

Fortunately, the mountain also kept the secret to recapturing the demons and defeating them for good. Deep inside it was a bottle gourd which radiated with every color of the rainbow. The old man managed to find it and retrieved a seed from it. When he got the seed, the mountain itself cracked open in half. He took the seed home and planted it. The next day, it had already grown into a bottle gourd vine.

The vine had grown seven bottle gourds on it, all of them of different colors. They grew at different speeds, but all were healthily growing and all had a unique color.

While the gourds grew, the demons rejoiced at their freedom, feasting on food taken from the villages. They also gathered other creatures and demons to join them. Every now and then, they would take on their serpent and scorpion form to terrorize the area further.

The snake-woman demon had a specific artifact that allowed her to summon magical weapons. One day, she used it to produce a mirror and scouted the land around her. Looking through her mirror, she saw the bottle gourd vine and how it was growing. The bottle gourd vine struck fear in her heart so she sent minions to attack it. A whole swarm of demon bees came to kill the vine with their poison, but one of the gourds, the green one, blew fire and killed them all.

The snake demon then sent a fire-breathing snake to attack them, but as it tried to burn the vine down, the blue gourd spouted water to save them.

The old man was watching from his window, and seeing the snake attack the vine, he went out to kill it. As soon as he left his house, the snake demon was there to capture him and take him away. None of the bottle gourds were ripe yet so they hung helplessly on the vine as the old man was dragged away.

The Red Bottle Gourd

The next day, the red bottle gourd shook viciously. Then with a loud crack, it tore in half and out came a red-dressed boy. He was the eldest of the children and was called Big Brother. All the bottle gourd children were strong, fast, and could jump high, but Big Brother was particularly strong and had a special ability that allowed him to change size, growing huge when he wanted to. Big Brother went to the nearby village and saw the destruction that raged. Everywhere there were bones and decay, and the farms and houses had all been burnt. He traveled past the villages into the mountains to attack the demons and bring back the old man. As soon as he came to the mountain, a big rock fell and tried to crush him, but he lifted it up and threw it away. He continued to wander the mountains until he spotted a cave. Inside, he found the scorpion and snake demons and told them to give back the old man or he would destroy their cave.

"You can't destroy our cave because your old man is here too," said the snake woman. "Let me take you to him and you can see him."

Big Brother, not being the brightest gourd, followed her. There he saw the old man lying on a stone table. He ran to the old man to bring him back home, but as soon as he touched the man, the old man disappeared and the whole place turned into quicksand. He was trapped and could not escape, nor were his powers any help.

The snake woman and scorpion man decided to keep the boy trapped to lure the rest of the children to them too, so that they could capture and kill all of them together.

The Orange Bottle Gourd

The next day, the orange gourd began to shake and out came an orange child. This child had supervision and hearing. Even from their house, he could see his trapped brother deep in the mountain. The orange child had to be much more careful and rely on his wits, since he had no real physical powers. He traveled to the mountains and lured the guards away with some treats. Once inside the cave, the second child looked for a way to get rid of the snake woman's artifact, but it was hidden away behind an impenetrable rock. Looking for a way to get past the rock, he traveled into a deep cavern where the snake woman had put up two giant mirrors. There, he was blinded by the reflections they caused. His eyes screamed in pain and then the snake demon came out and struck his ears too. No longer could he see or hear, and she threw him into prison with the old man.

The Yellow Bottle Gourd

In prison, they were found by a mole creature who dug them out of the mountain. The demons soon realized that the second brother and the old man had fled and pursued them. As the scorpion man caught up to recapture them, a yellow bottle gourd appeared. It still wasn't open. The scorpion demon tried to cut it in half, but instead that produced the yellow brother, whose superpower was invincibility. He easily withstood the scorpion man's attacks, allowing the second brother and the old man to escape home. The yellow brother attacked the scorpion man back, and his fingers shattered the scorpion's claws and sword. The demon fled, teleporting with a wisp of black smoke behind him. The third brother was not easily daunted, however, and chased after, back into the mountain. There he punched through the gates, his hands harder than any steel or iron. He found the mirror of the demons that had allowed them to see the gourd children growing on the vine and destroyed it.

The snake woman appeared, furious. She tried to attack the yellow child, but he laughed at her, letting her hit him with her sword.

"Bring out all your weapons. I will destroy them all," he said, laughing.

"If you can withstand three of my attacks, I will free your first brother and surrender," the snake demon said.

The boy laughed again. "Easy. Try your best." He bent his neck forward.

The snake woman brought out a new sword and struck him. Nothing happened.

"Is that the best you have?" the boy taunted. "You might as well surrender and give me my brother now."

She hit him again, but to no avail.

He laughed at her. "Last try."

This time the sword bent and turned into thousands of stringy swords, and rather than hit the third brother, they wrapped around him, tying him up. His invulnerability was no help against this, and the demons locked him up deep in the mountain.

The Green and Blue Bottle Gourd

The next day, two children were born, both the green and the blue one. The blue one immediately began watering the vine to ensure the others could keep growing. Once finished with this task, the two gourds turned to the task of freeing their brothers. This time, however, the old man cautioned them from going against the demons by themselves. Instead, they were to find herbs that could heal the second brother's hearing and sight. That way, they could get information on where the other brothers were now hidden and what the demons were doing.

The green and blue brothers headed out to look for herbs and saw the famine in the land. Everywhere, there was destruction and dry land. The blue child watered it, while the green one set fire to all the pests and snakes that were terrorizing the area.

Meanwhile, the demons were looking for an ancient magical pot that would allow them to destroy the bottle gourd children. Deep in a lake, they found the pot, but when they fished it out, it spurted fire and nearly destroyed them.

The two children saw the fire in the mountain and ran towards it. The blue brother quickly sent water at the flames to extinguish it, while the fire brother sucked some of it into himself. Then they saw the demons who were happy to have survived the fire.

"We must thank you, children," they said. "You have saved us."

"We can set you ablaze again," the green gourd child said.

"No need," the snake woman said, "why not let us thank you instead? We shall have a feast to celebrate this glorious day."

 "Release our brothers too."

"Of course, of course," the demons said.

The children were persuaded and followed the demons back to the mountain.

When they got to the mountain, the demons led them past a place where water blocked their path.

"We used to go across here, but it flooded yesterday," the snake woman said. "We will have to take the long way around."

"Nonsense," the blue brother said and opened his mouth and sucked the water into himself, allowing them to pass.

They arrived deep into the cave where the demons had a feast prepared.

"Your hall is very cold," the green fire child said. "I will fix that." Fire poured out of his mouth and all the torches and hearths were lit.

"You are both so impressive. Your skills rival that of the gods," the serpent demon said. "To celebrate your skills, let us drink wine together."

She produced a goblet filled with wine from her artifact and passed it to the green brother. He drained the glass and instantly began to wobble.

"The wine was cold," he slurred and then fell sound asleep.

"Brother!" the blue brother exclaimed.

"Wow, one glass of wine and he got drunk and fell asleep," the scorpion man mocked.

"Try me then!" the blue brother said. "Give me all your wine."

The scorpion demon and snake woman opened up all their barrels of wine, and the blue brother simply sat in his seat and summoned it all into his mouth. In a few moments, all their wine was gone.

"Huh, is that all you have? I hardly had time to taste the wine before it was gone," the blue brother said.

The scorpion demon was outraged. "He emptied all our wine!" The snake lady looked at the child, horrified, trying to think quickly of a new plan to fool the child. She asked her magical artifact for a new weapon to use and a massive bowl appeared. In the bowl was a new, sweet, fragrant wine.

"Mmm," the blue boy said, "that smells like wonderful wine."

"Let's make a deal then," the snake lady said. "If you can drain this bowl, we will give you anything you want."

"Easy," the water brother said and summoned the wine to him again. It flowed right into his open mouth. The bowl was emptied, and the blue brother began to sway. Before he could even look to see how much he had drunk, the bowl had refilled. He emptied it again and again until he finally collapsed, knocked out from all the alcohol.

The demons laughed, and the snake lady instantly took out her artifact to freeze the fire brother so that he would not be able to awaken and escape. The blue brother she enchanted and locked away in the deep wine bowl.

The Dark Blue Bottle Gourd

The next day, back at the house, birds flew in with the magical plant that the second brother needed to restore his sight and hearing. A few drops of nectar were dropped into his eyes and ears and suddenly his senses were restored. Just as this happened, an evil wind came and the demons appeared. The scorpion demon quickly attacked the old man and sent him tumbling off a cliff, while demonic bat minions attacked the second brother, capturing him with a net. The snake lady laughed and plucked the last two bottle gourds off the vine before they could hatch.

The demons quickly captured the second brother and brought everyone, including the unborn gourds, back to their cave and decided they would find a way to turn the bottle gourd children into an immortality potion. But two of the bottle gourds were still not ripe.

"Maybe we could grow them into our children," the snake demon said and placed the vine over a well of blackness and evil. But as soon as she did, the sixth bottle gourd jumped off the vine and cracked open.

But nothing appeared. Suddenly, the demons were being kicked and punched, before realizing that the child had the power of invisibility. The child ran away before they could find him.

Meanwhile, the old man, who had been thrown off a cliff, was awakened by an eagle. The bird took him on its wings and flew him to the bottle gourd mountain. There, the mountain spoke to him.

"You have awakened almost all of the seven bottle gourd children, but you forgot to take the Rainbow Lotus. Without it, they cannot combine their powers and defeat the demons. I will let you go back into me and find it. Take it to them and help them save the land."

"The children have already been destroyed by the demons. It's too late!" the old man said.

"They are not dead yet, merely captured. Go. Find the Rainbow Lotus and bring it to them."

A cloud appeared and the old man stepped onto it. It flew into the mountain and took him to its heart, where he could see a rainbow lotus flower waiting for him. He took it and was quickly transported out of the mountain.

During this time, the old man flew home on the eagle, Rainbow Louts in hand. He found the home destroyed, with none of the bottle gourds left. Instead, several demonic minions had been waiting for his arrival. They trapped him and took him back to the demons' cave.

Back in the demon's lair, the seventh brother was still in its gourd, hanging over the well of darkness. There the demons cultivated it, speaking to it and pouring evil ointments on it, trying to make it theirs.

Meanwhile, the dark blue brother explored the demons' mountain and found all of his brothers but couldn't free any of them. Finally, he found his second brother and asked for his help to find the snake lady's artifact.

"The scorpion demon is holding it," the second brother revealed. "He is asleep right now but might wake soon. It seems the demons always keep it on themselves."

"I will find a way to get it," the dark blue brother said.

The sixth brother was still sneaking around in the demons' mountain and found the scorpion demon feasting on wine and food. He used his invisibility and caused the demon to spill his meal multiple times. Then he teased and taunted the scorpion man. The demon was outraged and told all of his minions to catch him. The snake lady arrived and she too joined the chase. All of them tried to catch the dark blue child, but he evaded them, constantly changing where he was. Not even nets or frost worked to catch him, as he dodged them and instead made the snake demon accidentally freeze the scorpion man. As she had tried to freeze him, she had used the incantation needed to use the artifact. She quickly melted him, using the same incantation, which the dark blue brother heard. Both of the demons and their minions were outraged and looked everywhere for the dark blue child but could not find him.

Eventually, the demons had tired and went to sleep, holding their precious artifact in their hands. The dark blue brother waited until they were fast asleep. He took a leaf from his clothes and tickled it across the scorpion man's nose to make him sneeze. As the scorpion sneezed, he dropped the artifact he had been carefully holding. Before it hit the floor, the sixth child picked it up. He quickly ran to where all of his brothers were hidden and unfroze the green brother, released the yellow one from his ropes, and saved the others from their traps.

The Violet Bottle Gourd

The six brothers went to find the last violet brother who was encapsulated in a black prison, above a dark cauldron of evil.

"We are here to save you, brother!" they said.

"Brother? I don't have any brother. Go away or I'll call on Mummy!" he said, still inside his bottle gourd.

The brothers left him and started to attack the minions to find the demons and finally deal with them, once and for all.

However, the old man had finally arrived and was brought to the demons and the snake demon and scorpion man took him to see the seventh child. Just then, the violet child was born out of his bottle gourd. Unlike his brothers, his gourd did not break, but instead he was summoned out of it. The gourd shrunk and the child kept it in his hands for it was his power and weapon. He did not recognize the old man and announced his love for the snake woman, calling her mother.

"Child," she said, "we are being invaded by terrors that this man brought upon us."

"Don't worry, Mother," the boy said. "I will deal with them with my gourd."

Just then, the fourth and fifth brothers arrived.

"Release my brother and our grandpa to us," the green brother said. "Or I will spit fire at you."

"And I will drown you in water," the water brother shouted.

"Go away! How dare you attack this place?" their youngest brother shouted.

"You are confused, brother. Stop this madness," they told him.

"No, I will defend my mother and father!"

The green brother shot fire at them, but the violet brother soaked it all up into his gourd. The same happened again when the blue brother attacked with water. The violet brother was able to soak up everything and then returned fire with a spell from his gourd, causing the other two brothers to attack each other.

The red and yellow brother also arrived, but they too were made to attack each other. The violet brother then absorbed them into his bottle gourd, imprisoning them.

The orange and dark blue brother were also nearby, but were still hiding.

"I can deal with him. I still have this," the dark blue brother said, holding the demons' artifact. He went invisible and then uttered the incantation and sent it at his brother. But the seventh child's gourd absorbed it.

"Who attacks us now?" the seventh brother asked, outraged. "I will deal with them." He held out his bottle gourd and streams of water flowed out of it, finding the sixth and second brother and imprisoned them in the gourd too.

The old man openly cried. He remembered the beautiful vine he had planted with children full of potential and powers. "You have turned against your brothers," he said to the violet brother. "You don't remember anything of the care we have for you. I was your caretaker. Your grandpa."

At this, the violet brother started to cry. He could feel the truth of what the old man said and the grief resonated within him.

"He lies, child," the demons said, but there was anger in their voices.

"Mother," the violet child said, tears still in his eyes. "I have all the terrors in this bottle gourd. What do we do with them now?"

"Come, we must ensure that they never come back." The demons took the child and the old man to the pot they had found, the pot of eternal flames.

"Pour them into that," the snake demon said.

The violet boy did as he was told.

"Your bottle gourd truly is impressive," the snake lady said. "May I see it?"

"Only for a little while. It is mine," the boy said.

"Of course. I know it is yours. I would never keep it."

He handed her the gourd. Immediately, she pointed it at him and sucked him into it, before sending him into the pot of flames too.

The Rainbow Lotus

The pot burned before smoke suddenly steamed out of it and it ceased burning. Waves of water poured out and the pot stopped burning. Seeing this, the old man laughed.

"I will throw you into it too if you laugh again," the scorpion man said.

"You have caused your own failure," the old man said. "You divided the children so much that they cannot be formed into one pill of immortality and invincibility. But I can help you there. I can unite them so that they can be transformed."

"You?! Ha!" the scorpion demon mocked.

"Wait, let us see what the old man can do. What harm can it do?" the snake woman said.

At this, the old man took out the Rainbow Lotus and proclaimed, "With this the seven children can unite and become one to defeat you demons!" He threw the Rainbow Lotus toward the pot and it hovered above it, releasing drops of each color. With that, the seven boys were summoned out of the pot and into the lotus, before becoming their own size.

The demons quickly grabbed the old man, holding a knife to his throat.

"Don't hurt us or we will kill your beloved grandpa," they said.

"Don't worry about me. Just kill these demons!" the old man exclaimed.

The children hesitated and then the snake demon brought forth the youngest brother's bottle gourd.

"I will summon you back in, you terrible children!"

The old man pushed back against the scorpion demon which caught him off guard. He then lunged at the snake demon and made her drop the bottle gourd, which the violet brother quickly picked up. But before the brothers could react, the scorpion demon stabbed his blade into the back of the old man, killing him.

The brothers instantly started fighting together as one and used all of their superpowers against the demons. After the demons had been burnt, flooded, and crushed under rocks, the violet brother took out his bottle gourd and sucked them into it. As they were sucked in, the demons shrieked and shrunk into a tiny snake and scorpion. Finally, the brothers had united as one to defeat the demons and freed the land from their terror. The yellow brother split open a mountain and they locked the bottle gourd deep inside it. Then, the seven children were transformed into a rainbow mountain that stood on top of the bottle gourd. If the demons ever awaken, then so would the bottle gourd children.

Author's note:

This story is a much more recent construction from the 20th century, but uses many symbols and ideas that are taken and reshaped from mythology. The bottle gourd is traditionally thought to have healing powers in Chinese folklore; doctors have even used it to carry their medicinal herbs. It was also a symbol of Taoist immortals. This story not only uses this vegetable, but also combines it with very recognizable images, like the snake woman, who we know as Nüwa, only here she is evil. Besides this, it showcases the constant struggle between demons and humans and the importance of being careful not to disturb spirits. It also depicts the power in brotherhood and teamwork, rather than doing something by yourself.

Conclusion

Chinese mythology is as rich as it is diverse. These tales that you have read are just a selection of a vast ocean of stories, legends, and myths. This selection was made to give you a taste and hopefully leave you wanting more.

Chinese mythology is almost defined by the quest for immortality. Whether that is from Taoism, or if this idealism of immortality within Taoism stems from mythology, is hard to say. What is clear is that immortality is the greatest achievement in Chinese mythology. The gods that exist and the original Taoist pantheon became gods and achieved godhood through their action or deeds. There are, of course, exceptions to this, but they are few. Within Taoism, knowledge was the key to many things and helping other people with their knowledge of healing was especially honored.

With the arrival of Buddhism into China, immortality took a slight backseat, but the idea still remained. Buddhism brought in an element of self-control and self-denial, which is clear in the latter part of the Monkey King story. Suffering and serving penance is also emphasized.

Chinese Mythology continues to impact the society today with its ideas and ideals, even though a lot also has changed as China has become secularized. Today, you can buy the Monkey King as an ice cream and heroes from the Three Kingdoms are collectible trading cards. On a deeper level, the idea of teamwork and unity as is shown in the story of the bottle gourd children is highly cherished.

There are numerous legends, films and much more on Chinese Mythology, so if you now have a taste for a particular part of it and you want to know more, go and explore its deep caverns.

If you enjoyed this individual book on Chinese mythology, can you please leave a review for it?

Thanks for your support!

Part 2: Japanese Mythology

A Captivating Guide to Japanese Folklore, Myths, Fairy Tales, Yokai, Heroes and Heroines

Introduction

The study of mythology and folklore is a peculiar one to the extent that we are looking into things which are generally regarded as untrue yet critically important to a culture. We are also taking on the study of the "lore of the folk," and this faces us with the question of exactly which folk we are talking about. Japan, of course, is a single nation, but its origins are so old and often so fragmented that unified mythology and folklore can be difficult to point to. Still, in all, there are some key texts, tales, and characters we can focus on which will give us a pretty good sense of Japanese mythology.

Japanese culture offers a wealth of religious tradition, mythology, and stunning folklore. The earliest myths found in the two main religious books, the *Kojiki* and the *Nihon Shoki*, offer the obscure and often difficult stories of the earliest creation, the birth of the islands of Japan, and the ancestral lines of the Emperors. These texts, though distant to a contemporary reader at times, are filled with bizarre stories of the magic of gods. They offer numerous gods for everything in heaven and earth. The rules of the games they play can at times be difficult to understand. Even the importance of numbers can get confusing, yet there is a logic to these texts. There is an elaborate code of conduct and an exhaustive lineage which is designed to take the reader up to the historical emperors of Japan.

It is probably important to remember as we work our way through these books that, though these are the oldest texts in Japanese mythology, they are nonetheless an amalgam of Chinese and Indian lore which found its way to Japan and mingles into the earliest beliefs of ancient Japan. If the going gets confusing, it is because the stories themselves are confusing. However, like all mythological systems, it is perhaps a mistake to try to assign a very human logic to the thoughts and actions of deities which precede humanity.

The *Kojiki* and the *Nihon Shoki* are the holy texts of the Shinto religion which pervades Japan to this day. Though we can read these texts as mythology and folklore, they are also read by some as religious texts. The *Kojiki* and the *Nihon Shoki* are the earliest stories which came to form the Shinto religion.

Before delving into the *Kojiki* and the *Nihon Shoki*, it is helpful to survey the basic ideas of the Shinto religion. Shinto is believed to be the indigenous religion and tradition of Japan. As we will see, one of the most critical features of Shinto is ancestor worship, but this is tied to worship of the kami, or, roughly translated, the deities. Since Shinto reveres the natural world as a feature of divine creation, we find kami in every aspect of life and nature. At one time, kami were venerated and worshiped just about anywhere and everywhere. Now one will find jinja, or designated temples specifically for worshiping specific kami.

Kami

Since ancient times, Japanese culture has involved tremendous respect and awe for nature and all features of the natural world. For this reason, just about all aspects of nature are associated with specific kami. So, there is the sun, the moon, and the earth, and there are kami which correspond to each of these. As we will see in the central books which form the basis of Shinto beliefs and practices, there are kami for every aspect of life and death. Those who attend death are ugly and terrifying. But this should not lead us to believe that the kami associated with life are completely benign. Shinto religion accepts that nature is capricious and dangerous. What gives us life is the very thing which takes it away. Kami do not exist simply to please humanity and make life peaceful and easy. The kami of the Shinto religion animates all aspects of life and are therefore an essential feature of things which are unpleasant. The Shinto religion seems to accept that one must take the bitter with the sweet.

Jinja

Throughout the *Kijiki*, for example, we find points in the stories which designate specific geographical locations as the sites where the deities performed certain functions. The gateway to the underworld exists as a real geographic site. Elsewhere, the forms of the kami designate areas for worship and for performing rituals. At one-time, evergreen trees, for example, were decorated to worship and revere kami of nature, and for performing sacred rituals. Over time these areas have been marked by shrines called Jinja. These are primarily temples dedicated to specific kami. They are the familiar pavilion-style structures so closely associated with Japanese culture.

Beyond these ancient texts which remain significant as religious texts to this day, Japanese culture offers a wealth of other mythological stories. The yokai are Japan's fairies and elves. These creatures are difficult to pin down because they are just as inconsistent in their habits and ways as the fairies and elves from other parts of the world.

Yokai can often be extremely dangerous and the three we will look at are the most dangerous. Yokai can be transformed into oni, or demons, at which point they become malevolent and destructive. Other Yokai are merely indifferent creatures who inhabit a space which seems to be just adjacent to our world. They come and go without causing much of a problem unless they perceive a wrong on the part of the human world. As we will see, as much as Japan keeps the lore of the evilest yokai, there is also those Yokai who grant wishes as well.

In addition to these mythological realms, Japan also has its store of fairy tales. The fairy tales of Japan follow themes which are at once familiar and strange. The figure of the dragon looms large in Japanese fairy tales and dragons are not necessarily the fearsome creatures we know from western traditions. Dragons hold a different place in Japanese lore. They are at times quite gentle; other times they hold the position of the highest royalty.

As with the fairy tales we are accustomed to, the Japanese tradition includes tales of simple wonder and magic, and tales designed to teach lessons to children. We will look at just couple of these stories.

Finally, we will look at a hero and heroine from the Japanese mythological tradition. England has it King Arthur, the Greeks had Achilles, and the Romans had Ulysses. The Japanese tradition has characters which serve similar cultural functions. As with the other aspects of Japanese mythology, there are differences from the western myths we may be more accustomed to. But the heroes we will look at are just as brave and majestic in ways which serve the Japanese ideals of heroism.

Chapter 1 – Introduction to the *Kojiki*

One of the most important texts in the mythology of Japan, indeed, possibly the central text for Japanese spiritual culture is the *Kojiki* or *The Record of Ancient Matters*. First compiled in the 8th Century (711-712 CE), the *Kojiki* is the text of the ancient Shinto religion and the spiritual beliefs which underpin it. The creation myths, the stories which have shaped mythology in Japan originate in the *Kojiki*. The origins of the Emperors is found in this text. The Emperors of Japan found their roots in the Gods who gave rise to the islands of Japan.

There are three main sections to the *Kojiki*. The first is the *Kamitsumaki*. This contains the preface to the *Kojiki* and the stories of the Age of the Gods. It also includes the creation stories—the creation and founding of Japan and the origin of the Emperors. The second section, the *Nakatsumaki*, begins with the story of the first Emperor, Jimmu. This recounts his conquest of Japan and takes the reader up to the 15th Emperor, Ojin. Finally, the text traces the reigns of the 16th through 33rd Emperors in what is titled *Shimotsumaki*. The third and final section shows limited interaction between the human world and the gods.

The *Kojiki* mixes the realms of human and divine in a manner we recognize from other mythological systems. The Judeo-Christian bible offers numerous tales of these interactions between humans and God. The Greeks and Romans built their entire modes of belief and their entire myth structure out of the dialogue between Gods and humans. The *Kojiki* follows a similar pattern with the gods receding from intimate contact with the human realm the closer we get to recorded history.

The *Kojiki*, like most other great texts of ancient origins, has a clouded history. Most scholars agree that much of the text is cribbed from Chinese mythology to the extent that China exerted a tremendous influence on early Japanese culture. Until roughly the 8th Century, most of the myths and legends of Japan were kept privately by individual families. It was the Emperor Temmu in 681 who became adamant on compiling these myths and legends into one text. It laid dormant for twenty-five years before finally being completed. No matter the various sources, the central place of the *Kojiki* to modern Japanese culture and modern Shinto practice cannot be denied. The *Kojiki* stands as a Japanese text.

The Creation Stories

Like nearly all mythological systems, the *Kojiki* begins with the creation myths. The text begins with the creation of seven deities. Most agree that the crux of the creation myth begins with the brother and sister gods, Izanagi and Izanami, who set in motion the birth of the lands and the peoples who would come. We are told this brother and sister are granted a heavenly jeweled spear which they dip into the briny water. When they pull the spear up, it drips the brine onto the oil which was the primal space before the creation of the earth until an island was formed: "This is the Island of Onogoro," as the text explains.

From here the *Kojiki* relates the creation of natural forces such as the sun, the moon, and fire all who are enlivened by attendant gods and goddesses. Most notable of these are the Sun Goddess and her brother, Susano-o, and the conflicts between the two of them. Susano-o is seen as the rebel in the text, analogous to other rebels in mythology such as Loki in the Norse tradition. He is also referred to as being evil which would make him something like the devil except that Japanese tradition consists of other demon characters. It is from Susano-o that the Emperors dynasties are traced.

The next two sections are more generally concerned with the vast genealogies of royal lines. Beginning with the supernatural beings and tales, the *Kojiki* recounts the rise of the mythological Emperor and Empress Jimmu and Sojin. We read of the rise of the mythological heroes Yamato-Take and Jin-go. In all, the text traces the genealogies of 17 Emperors over many centuries.

There is an entire literature of scholarship on the *Kojiki,* and you could spend your life studying this text. The importance of this book cannot be stressed enough since it is one of the founding texts of both the Shinto religion and the origin of Japanese national identity.

For the western reader, it is easy to get confused while reading the *Kojiki*. The names are unfamiliar, and some of the features of the mythology are unknown to us. There is a strange significance to the number eight, whereas in the Judeo-Christian tradition it is the number seven. The tremendous importance Izanami places on her shame may be foreign to some readers. However, there are numerous points of reference which will be quite familiar. The mysterious beginnings of the deities are strikingly similar to the unfathomable origins of gods in other myths. The tension between the heavens, the earth, and the underworld are all familiar to us. And the tricky intelligence of the hero, Susano-o, should come as no surprise.

Since the *Kojiki* contains such a vast amount of information, including long genealogies of Emperors, it is helpful to focus on a few of the mythologies included in the text. Of interest is the ancient Japanese story of Creation and Origins and the rise of Susano-o, the great hero, and trickster of the *Kojiki*.

The Myths of Origins

Before Creation, the Center of Heaven Deity and The Reproducing Deity existed in the Plain of High Heaven. Next Came the Wondrous Reproducing Deity. These Deities lived alone when all creation consisted of the Earth and the Sea. The Earth and the Sea were unformed and existed as an oil. The *Kojiki* explains that the Earth and Sea floated medusa-like over the oil. Next came the Pleasant-Reed-Shoot-Prince-Elder-Deity and the Heavenly-Eternally-Standing-Deity. This leads to the time of The Seven Divine Generations which first are the Earthly-Eternally-Standing-Deity and the Luxuriant-Integrating-Master-Deity. What follows are the Mud-Earth-Lord and his sister Mud-Earth-Lady. Next appear the Germ-Earth-Integrating –Deity and his sister Life-Integrating-Deity. Finally, the order of the original Deities are as follows: Elder-of-the-Great-Place and his sister Elder-Lady-of-the-Great-Place; Perfect-Exterior and his sister Oh-Awful-Lady; Male-Who-Invites and his sister Female-Who-Invites. These are the generations of the Deities who precede the creation of the world.

With all the Deities assembled it is commanded that Male-Who-Invites, Izanagi, and his sister Female-Who-Invites, Izanami, are to give birth to a drifting island. These are the two principle created deities. They are given a jeweled spear. The two deities stand on the Floating Bridge of Heaven and plunge the jeweled spear into the brine of the unformed sea. Upon withdrawing the spear, the brine drips down and forms the island of Onogoro which means "self-condensed." This is the origin of the first creation. The islands which would come to make up Japan are derived from this moment in the *Kojiki*.

The Journey to the Underworld

After the creation of the islands and the things in the world, Izanami gave birth to the fire god, Kagutsuchi. In the process, she was burned terribly and eventually died from her injuries. Izanagi buried her on Mt. Hiba and her spirit descended to Yomi-no-kuni which is the underworld.

After Izanami was gone, Izanagi missed her and decided to go find her. He traveled to Mt. Hiba and found the gates of Yomi-no-kuni. Izanami's spirit greeted him at the gates. Izanagi told her they were not finished with the creation of the world. He wanted her to come back with him, but she told him she had already eaten of the food of the earth and could no longer leave. She contemplates her brother's visit and words and says that since he has traveled all this way she could talk to the lord of this world. She explains that Izanagi must wait. She explicitly tells him that he must not look at her.

After some time has passed, Izanagi became impatient. Breaking a tooth off the comb he had in his hair, he made a torch to light his way and pursued her. He entered Yomi-no-kuni and found her rotting. She was crawling with maggots. Eight gods of thunder hung from her body. Izanagi was terrified and fled. Izanami told him: "I told you not to look at me. You have caused me great shame." With this, she ordered the evil hags of the underworld to chase him.

Izanagi ran, but the hags started to catch up to him. In desperation, he threw a band from his hair onto the ground which changed into a grapevine full of grapes. This slowed the hags as they paused to eat the grapes, but they ate faster than Izanagi had hoped, and they quickly caught up with him. This time, he broke another tooth from his comb and threw it on the ground where bamboo shoots sprung forth. The hags paused to eat the bamboo shoots and again they were slowed in their pursuit of Izanagi.

Izanami, seeing that Izanagi would escape, ordered the gods of thunder and an army of evil spirits to chase him. Izanagi pulled out his sword and swung at his attackers but to no avail. He ran on. As he approached the gates of the underworld, he came upon a peach tree. Plucking three peaches, he hurled them at his attackers and drove them back into the underworld.

This time, Izanami herself went after him. Izanagi took a giant boulder and blocked the entrance to Yomi-no-kuni, forever separating the underworld from the earth and himself from Izanami. Here they said their final farewells.

Izanami pronounced a curse: Everyday she would kill one thousand people from the world for the shame Izanagi has caused her. Izanagi replied that in return, he would 'people the earth' with five thousand inhabitants. They never saw each other again.

Izanagi bathed himself to remove the filth of the underworld. In doing this, many new deities were born. Of these, the sun goddess, Amaterasu, came forth as Izanagi washed his left eye. From his right eye, Tsukuyomi, the deity of the moon was born.

Izanagi loved his children and gave them each a realm. Amaterasu was given the heavens. To Tsukuyomi, he gave the night. A third deity, Susano-o, who came into being as Izanagi washed his nose, was given the seas.

These new deities were happy with their realms. However, Susano-o was rebellious. He acted out against Izanagi. For this, he was banished to the Earth.

The Wanderings of Susano-o

After he was banished to earth, Susano-o found himself wandering up the river Hii to the land of Izumo. He noticed some chopsticks floating down the river and decided to see who may have lost them. He finally came upon an elderly couple and their daughter, Kushinada-hime. The couple were crying in despair, and Susano-o asked them why. They explained that their daughter was to be sacrificed to the serpent monster, Yamata-no-Orochi. This monster was foul, with eight heads and eight tails; its body long enough to cover eight mountain peaks. It was covered with moss and trees, and its underside was inflamed and smeared with blood.

Susano-o further discovered that the couple initially had eight daughters, all of whom had been sacrificed to Yamata-no-Orochi each year until they were only left with Kushinada-hime. Susano-o told the couple that if they gave him their daughter's hand in marriage, he would slay the serpent. To which they happily agreed.

Susano-o set about his preparations. He first turned Yamata-no-Orochi into a comb and placed her in his hair. Next, he instructed the couple to brew some strong sake. They were to build a fence around the house with eight gates. He then instructed them to build a platform and place a vat filled with the sake inside each gate. After the preparations were complete, he told them to wait.

Susano-o knew that serpents loved sake, and as he expected, each of the serpent's eight heads dipped into all eight vats of sake and drank until the serpent was quite drunk. It soon passed out from being drunk.

Susano-o watched from his safe hiding place. As soon as he saw the Yamata-no-Orochii was drunk and passed out, he sprang from his spot and cut the serpent to pieces until the river Hii ran red with its blood.

As Susano-o was cutting the serpent's tail, he struck something which broke his blade. As he examined the cut, he discovered a sword. He quickly realized this was no ordinary sword. Seeing its importance, Susano-o offered the sword to his sister, Amaterasu, the deity of the sun and ruler of the heavens. The sword was called Kusunagi-no-tsurugi, or the Great Sword of Kusunagi. This became one of the three great Imperial Treasures of Japan.

Having slain the hideous serpent Yamata-no-Orichi, and finding Kushinada-himi safe, Susano-o began searching for a place suitable to build a palace. After a time, he arrived in Suga. Here he decided this was the place where he felt at peace, and he built his palace. Soon after, a large cloud appeared. Susano-o looked up at the sky and recited his poem:

Izumo is a land protected by clouds aplenty

And like this land of Izumo

I shall build a fence to protect the palace

Where my wife will live

Like the clouds in the land of Izumo

With this, Susano-o appointed his father-in-law, Ashinazuchi, to be caretaker of the place. Susano-o and Kushinada-himi lived in the palace at Suga. It is believed that the poem Susano-o recited is the origin of traditional Japanese poetry such as waka and haiku.

Chapter 2 – Introduction to the *Nihon Shoki*

In addition to the *Kojiki,* the other central text in Japanese religion and spirituality is the *Nihon Shoki*. This text contains many of the same tales concerning the origins of the world and the gods, but it provides some alternative stories that offer more details on the lives and adventures of the gods and early heroes and heroines.

The primary significance of the *Nihon Shoki* is the lengthy genealogies which provide the origins of royal dynasties and the divine origins of the Emperors. Whereas this information occupies mainly the last two-thirds of the *Kojiki*, the details of critical genealogical lines would appear to be the primary focus and purpose of the *Nihom Shoki*. Nevertheless, this text does contain a wealth of mythological material.

In the *Nihon Shoki,* we encounter the same mythological figures. Izanami and Izanagi are present, and their importance to the birth of Japan are identical. Some of the other characters are slightly different. The birth of the sun, moon, and various features of the earth are detailed in the *Nihon Shoki,* and we will explore some of these stories. We will encounter the hero and troublemaker Susano-o, only in this text, he appears as Susawono. It is the same trickster figure from the *Kojiki*.

The Birth of Amaterasu, Trukuyumi, Susawono, and the Leech-Child

Each of these tales is broken into various versions. Apparently, the oral tradition from which this text was compiled, pulled together a wide variety of source material. One may conjecture that the earliest scribes of the *Nihon Shoki* deemed all versions of the tale to be worthy of preservation and study. For this reason, they preserved and transcribed the repetition we find in the collection of stories. The following summary is from Section Five, Main Version.

After they have made way for the creation of the Earth and the islands of Japan, Izanami and Izanagi made the sea, the rivers, and the mountains. They gave birth to Kukunochi, the ancestor of the trees and Kusanohime, the ancestor of the grass, who is also called Notsuchi.

Izanami and Izanagi spoke to each other and said: "We have already given birth to the eight-island country, its rivers, its trees, and its grasses; why don't we give birth to rulers of this country." At which they gave birth to Ohirume no Muchi who is also called Amaterasu. This is the sun goddess.

The child was so bright that she shined on every quarter of Japan. Izanami and Izanagi rejoiced at their daughter, and they said "Though our breaths have been many, we have yet to make one to equal this child. She should not reside in this country. She should be sent to heaven, and she should be given heavenly duties." Using the pillar of the earth, they sent her to heaven.

After this, they gave birth to the moon god who is called Tsukuyomi no Mikoto. He shone brightly like his sister and was sent to heaven.

They then gave birth to the leech-child. Even as he reached the age of three, his legs would not allow him to stand. He was placed in a boat of hardened camphor and cast to the winds.

The next born was Susawono no Mikoto. In another version, he is called Kamususanowo no Mikoto. Susawono no Mikoto was brazen and committed many acts of disrespect. He also had a habit of frequently weeping and wailing. He caused many people in the country to die. He once caused two green mountains to wither. For this, Izanami and Izanagi banished him from their realm. He was sent to distant Nenokuni.

The Story of the Comb and the Curse

The story of Izanami and Izanagi in which she is transformed into an ugly demon and the subsequent journey into the underworld is re-told in *Nihon Shoki* with some differences. It is worth presenting this alternative version since this tale is central to the mythological Traditions of Japan.

Izanagi followed Izanami to the land of Yomi. When they spoke, Izanami told him "Why have you come so late? I have already eaten the food of this world. I must rest so; please do not look at me." Izanagi would not listen. He took his comb out of his hair and broke off a tooth. With this, he made a torch. When he looked at her, she was horrifying. Pus spurted from her and maggots crawled on her. For this reason, people to this day hate to carry a single torch at night and refuse to throw a comb on the ground.

Izanagi exclaimed "I have unknowingly visited a polluted land," and he quickly ran away. Izanami said with shame and remorse "Why didn't you listen to me? Now you have put me to shame." With this, she let loose the eight ugly women of Yomi to pursue him and trap him in Yomi.

Izanagi pulled out his sword. Swinging it behind him as he fled. He threw away his black headpiece, and it was transformed into grapes. The eight ugly women stopped to eat the grapes. When they were finished, the continued to pursue him. Izanagi then threw down his comb, and it was transformed into bamboo shoots. Again, the eight ugly women stopped to eat the bamboo shoots and then quickly pursued him. Finally, Inzanagi pursued Izanami herself, but at this time he was already at the border of Yomi and the living word.

At the border of Yomi, Izanagi lifted a giant boulder just as the women were approaching him. Izanagi took the rock and blocked the exit from Yomi. He pronounced the oath of divorce from Izanami.

Izanagi told him "If you say this oath I will strangle 1,000 people from this world every day you are a ruler." In response, Izanagi said "If you do such a thing I will cause 1,500 children to be born every day. Do not come beyond this point. He threw down his staff, called Funato no Kami; then he threw down his belt, called Nagachiha no Kami; then he threw down his robe called Wazurahi no Kami; then he threw down his pants, which are called Akikuhi no Kami; then he threw down his shoes, called Chishiki no Kami. The boulder remains to block the passage to the underworld.

[The passage to the underworld may not actually be a physical space, but rather, a state or period between when you stop breathing and when you actually die].

Amaterasu and Susanowo

This is from Section Five, Version Twelve. The book adds multiple versions, but this is the central tale.

Izanagi decided to appoint his three children to rule the various plains. Amaterasu, the sun, should govern the heavens, Tsukiyomi, the moon, should assist in ruling the heavens. And Susanowo would be the ruler of the seas.

Amaterasu said from the heaven that she had heard that in the plain country below lives Ukemochi no Kami. She told Tsukiyomi to go and see. Tsukiyomi went to the earth to find the origin of Ukemochi no kami who then turned his head to face the country. As he did, grain came out of his mouth. He then turned toward the sea and all the fish, large and small, came out of his mouth. When Ukemochi no Kami turned toward the mountains, all the animals of the earth came out of his mouth. Ukemochi no kami then prepared food and placed it on 100 tables.

Tsukiyomi became angry and declared, "Filthy and vile! You should offer up things that come out your mouth to me." Tsukiyomi then drew his sword and killed Ukemochi no Kami. When he returned to heaven and reported this to Amaterasu, she became angry and told him he was an evil god and she could not look at him. The two spent one day and one night apart.

Amaterasu then sent another god, Amano Kumahito to investigate the matter. However, Ukemochi no Kami was already dead, yet, from the crown of his head came cows and horses. Millet grew from his forehead and silkworms sprung from his eyebrows. More millet came from his eyes and rice came from his stomach. From his genitals grew wheat and beans. Amano Kumahito collected all these things and brought them in offering to Amaterasu.

Amaterasu was happy with this. She saw that the people of the earth could eat and cultivate them. The millet, wheat, and beans would grow in the fields. The rice would fill the rice paddy. She then appointed a village chief in heaven. The chief began to plant and cultivate everything. Ameratasu put the silkworms in her mouth and reeled the thread and from this arose sericulture.

The Contract of Amaterasu and Susawono

The sun goddess knew of the evil purposes of her brother Susawono and was prepared for him. When he came to her in heaven, she made defenses with a ten, a nine, and an eight-span sword. She also carried a holy arrow and a quiver of arrows. She was confident he was coming to steal her heavenly plane, and she met him in heaven to defend herself.

Susanowo said to her, "In the beginning, I was not evil, and I was pure of heart. I came only to see my sister for a short time. Amaterasu replied, "If you have good intentions then you will birth children."

Then Amaterasu ate all three of her swords and gave birth to three goddesses, one for each sword.

In response to this, Susanowo took a necklace of 500 beads of jade from his sister. He rinsed it in the Nuna well of heaven, and he ate the necklace. He then gave birth to five male gods. Amaterasu then knew that Susanowo was pure of heart. In return, she sent the three goddesses to earth to tend to the people of the earth. The place where she sent them is called Tsukushi and is revered for this to this day.

Chapter 3 – Influence and Importance of the *Kojiki* and *Nihon Shoki* to Indigenous Japanese Religion

Japanese religion as it is practiced today is largely a mix of Buddhism and Shinto. The *Kojiki* exerts its influence as something of a dogmatic text. It operates on the order of the Holy Bible in that it lays the groundwork for Japanese religious practices.

The Japanese tradition which comes out of the *Kojiki* is one of ancestor worship. Throughout the *Kojiki* we see ancestral lineages traced out. Even in the showdowns between the sun goddess and Susanowo (or Susno-o, depending on which text we read), we witness a heavy emphasis on ancestors and lineages. Shinto practices and beliefs still venerate ancestral lines as an integral part of their religious system.

The long line of deities which are given in detail in the first book of the *Kojiki* shows us the importance of ancestors. As the gods split and reproduce, the line of descent is carefully delineated.

We should also pay attention to the distinctly patriarchal qualities of these systems. We do, however, still see deeply cherished female deities and figures. Though the male line may be the favored line, the tradition found in the *Kojiki* places great value on the female.

Since Shinto religious ideals focus on the ancestor worship and the male lineage, it should not come as a shock that there is a cult of the phallus in the Japanese mythology. The holy shrines of ancient Japan, and to a lesser extent, contemporary Japan, all contain phallic symbols. It is easy to read this wrong as western readers as many other cultures also use phallic symbols. This is not a prurient deification of the phallus. Rather, phallic symbols are holy images of the ancestral lines which are passed down through the male lineage. Even the creation myth contains the image of a spear which is dipped into the brine and then drips the seeds of the earth. These are the kinds of phallic images which are held to be divine in ancient Japanese mythology.

Chapter 4 – Yokai

In addition to such an essential and unifying text like the *Kojiki*, Japanese mythology and folklore are rich in tales of mysterious and magical creatures collectively referred to as Yokai. The Yokai range from malevolent creatures who cause suffering and misfortune, to the merely mischievous who create havoc, to those who bring good fortune and blessings.

Much of Japanese folk tradition is an amalgam of different traditions that have found their way into the lore of Japanese culture. Though changed and suited to fit the unique Japanese traditions and further modified by Shinto and later Buddhist practices, at least some of the origins of the yokai are in Chinese and Indian lore.

Though the *Kojiki* does contain stories of magic, the supernatural, and demons, it stands as a distinct tradition from Yokai tales. Much of Yokai stories are contained in diverse sources. There is no central unifying text such as we see in the *Kojiki*.

During the Edo period (1603-1868), Japan underwent an unprecedented time of artistic and cultural growth. There was an upswing in interest in ghost stories and tales of the supernatural that contained demons and benevolent magical creatures. Toriyama Sekien is a pivotal figure in this cultural moment. He recorded a large body of the oral tradition and compiled this in illuminated scrolls. These became a multi-volume encyclopedia of Japanese folktales and folklore. In doing this, he opened the way for other artists to follow suit and the boom in Japanese folktales began. The legacy of the Yokai in the broader Japanese imagination is one of the central features of Toriyama Sekien's work.

Stories of the Yokai fell out of favor as Japan sought to modernize in the 20th century. However, recent years has seen a resurgence of popularity for Yokai. They are now collected in numerous volumes. They have been illustrated in graphic novels and Japanese anime. These sorts of stories which include fantastic creatures, horrifying and beautiful, are readily accessible to animators and modern story-tellers.

Yokai come in myriad forms and types. They are analogous to the faery folk in many ways, and like the faery, they range in importance. Among the Yokai, there are three that are widely considered to be the evilest of all. Shuten-doji, Tamamo no Mae, and Sutoku are considered to be so evil that they are held responsible for plunging the entire nation of Japan into chaos and ruin.

The Three Most Evil Yokai of Japan

Shuten-doji

Before he attained his status as a legendary monster, Shuten-doji was believed to be a simple, if troublesome, orphan child. He had a reputation for being extremely intelligent and strong; so much so that many people believed his father must have been a demon of some sort, or possibly even a dragon. At a young age, Shuten-doji was sent to be a monk. However, he was not well-suited to monastic life. He treated his superior, and others, with disrespect. He got into fights. Most notably, he had a taste for sake and drank frequently and heavily. This is how he got the name Shuten-doji, which means "little drunkard."

On one night, Shuten-doji got drunk and decided to play some pranks at a festival. He put on an oni mask, a demon face, and crept around the festival jumping out and scaring people. After he was through, much satisfied with himself, he sneaked away and tried to take off the oni mask. It would not come off. It seemed that the oni mask had become fused to his face. It was now part of his body.

When he returned to the monks, he was teased and ridiculed for how ugly he had become. He was even punished for his pranks and told how evil he was. For this, he started to become like an oni deep inside. His heart grew corrupt, and he became full of anger. He finally fled the monks up into the mountains to live as a hermit.

In his isolation and solitude, Shuten-doji began to hate the world. He came to embrace his own evil and studied black magic. He started to use his intelligence and his new-found evil powers to attack travelers and merchants. He even kidnapped young men and women, and it is said that he drank their blood and ate their organs.

After some time, other demons and evil creatures were attracted to him. He began to amass an army of oni and evil people. As these others spent time with Shuten-doji they too were transformed into oni.

Eventually, Shuten-doji and his army built a castle on Mt. Oe. He plotted his vengeance on the world of people. He sought to become king of Japan.

Shuten-doji began to attack the Emperor of Japan. Using his mountain castle as a base, he began his attempt to take over and continued to attack more and more. The kidnappings and murders also persisted. Shuten-doji had launched a reign of terror. Eventually, Emperor Ichijo decided that Shuten-doji and his oni army must be stopped.

The Emperor sent his bravest warrior, Raiko, to climb Mt. Oe and bring back the head of Shuten-doji. Raiko and his men headed into the mountains. There they found the oni army inside their castle drinking sake. Raijo and his men poisoned the sake and put the oni army into a deep sleep. Raiko and his men were able to sneak into the castle.

They attacked the oni and killed them one by one. Finally, they made their way to Shuten-doji. Raiko sliced off the oni jing's head. However, even in death, Shuten-doji was so powerful that his head bit at Raiko and his men. In the end, they buried Shuten-doji's head outside the city where it would cause no more trouble.

[There are many versions of the Shuten-doji tale. His malevolent influence and ruinous legacy is an essential myth in Japanese culture and history. One of the most famous is part of a more extensive work called *Ehon Hyaku Monogatari*. This is an illuminated text which contains a full treatise on Yokai in general. We may see this as an old forerunner of the manga we are familiar with today.

The Story of Tamamo no Mae

Tamamo no Mae is one of the most notorious yokai in Japanese folklore. There are numerous stories about her, and she turns up in Chinese and Indian traditions also. She is beautiful but horrifying. Leading orgies and murderous rampages everywhere she goes, she is the sower of discord in every tale associated with her.

Unlike Shuten-doji, Tamamo no Mae was evil by her very nature. She began as a shape-shifting fox with nine tails. Her evil and her ambition were unmatched in the world. At one time, she disguised herself as a human child and was taken in by an elderly couple who could not have their own child. This couple raised her as their own and named her Mikuzume.

As a young girl, Mikuzume showed herself to be exceptionally talented and bright. For these reasons, she attracted the attention of nearly everyone. So gifted was she that at the age of seven she was invited to recite poetry for the Emperor Toba who was so taken by her that he offered her a position as a servant in the imperial court.

Mikuzume quickly became a star at the court. She absorbed knowledge unlike anyone before. There was not a single thing that was beyond her. She excelled at music, history, astronomy, religion and Chinese classics. She was stunningly beautiful, and even her clothes were perfect. She smelled lovely. Everyone who laid eyes on her instantly fell in love with her.

During a poetry recital, one summer, a powerful rainstorm struck, and the winds blew out all the candles in the recital chamber. Suddenly, much to the astonishment of everyone, a mysterious light began to emanate from Mikuzume's body. The people in the audience were stunned and dismayed. Someone declared that Mikuzume must have had a holy life in a past life and she was given the name of Tamamo no Mae. Emperor Toba, who was already smitten by the girl, invited her to be his royal consort.

Not long after this, the Emperor Toba became ill. The emperor's court brought in the most learned physicians. None could determine what was wrong. They brought in high priests and sorcerers—they consulted every source they could to determine the cause of the emperor's illness. No one could figure it out. The sorcerers suggested that someone close to the emperor was making him sick and there were those who suspected Tamamo no Mae. They suggested that she was a fox in disguise and that she was using magic to make the emperor ill. But the emperor was so blinded by love that he refused to listen to these concerns. In fact, it was Tamamo no Mae. She was using her evil magic to shorten the emperor's life.

It was decreed that a divine ritual would be necessary to save the life of the emperor. Tamamo no Mae was ordered to participate. The sorcerers who suspected her knew if she was forced to recite the magic ritual, her evil magic would be revealed. Tamamo no Mae also knew this, but given her position, she had no choice but to go through with the magic rituals. All went well for Tamamo no Mae even as she recited the holy words. However, just as she was about to finish the ceremony and wave the magic staff to complete it, she vanished from sight. Thus, the sorcerer's suspicions were confirmed.

The emperor, furious over the betrayal, summoned his finest warriors and assembled an army of 80,000 men to hunt down and kill Tamamo no Mae. Reports came in that one of the warriors had spotted a nine-tailed fox in the east. Tamamo no Mae was chased and hunted all the way to the plains of Nasuno.

Just before the army caught up to her, Tamamo no Mae appeared to one of the emperor's men to plead for her life. His name was Miuranosuke. She cried and told him that on the next day he would find her and kill her. She begged him to spare her. Her beauty enchanted him, and her cries moved him to pity. But he was a man of great honor, and he rejected her.

The next day, as foretold by Tamamo no Mae, Miuranosuke saw a nine-tailed fox. He shot two arrows at it and pierced the fox in the side and the neck. Another soldier, Kazusanosuke, swung his sword at the fox's head. Tamamo no Mae fell dead. The army returned to the emperor with the body of the fox as proof they had killed Tamamo no Mae.

However, Tamamo no Mae's evil power persisted even after her death. The great emperor of Japan died without an heir. Emperor Toba died shortly after this. The crisis of authority plunged Japan into chaos. Thus, this crisis of power marked the beginning of the rise of the shoguns.

Emperoro Sutoku, or Sutoku Tenno

It is officially recorded that Emperor Sutoku was the eldest child of Emperor Toba. However, it is also widely known and accepted that he was, in fact, the offspring of Emperor Toba's father, Emperor Shirakawa. Though Emperor Shirakawa was retired, he still held considerable power and influence over matters of the court and pulled the strings where real decisions were concerned. Emperor Shirakawa forced Emperor Toba to abdicate in favor of his son, Sutoku, who was younger and who the older Emperor could control much easier than Toba.

Upon the death of Shirakawa, Toba assumed the power of the throne. Since Toba considered Sutoku to be an illegitimate bastard, he began his revenge by convincing him to appoint Toba's son as his successor. Toba's son, Konoe, was only three years old and consequently, he was a puppet of his father, Emperor Toba. With this in place, Emperor Toba forced all of Sutoku's followers to be transferred to distant provinces, and he staffed the capital with people loyal to Toba.

Emperor Konoe was a sickly child and he died young, at the age of 17. With this, a power struggle ensued between Toba's next oldest son and the son of Sutoku. By this time, the court was stacked with supporters of Emperor Toba and his son, Go-Shirakawa became next in line.

The following year, Toba died. Sutoku's followers attempted to take back the throne from Go-Shirakawa, and a bloody struggle ensued. The rebellion was defeated and Go-Shirakwa's revenge was merciless. He had all of Sutoku's followers executed along with their families, and Sutoku was banished to Sanuki.

Sutoku lived out his life in exile. He lived as a monk, shaved his head and spent his days copying by hand the holy sutras. After many years of work, he sent his scrolls to Kyoto as an offering for the imperial temples. Go-Shirakawa suspected Sutoku had cursed the scrolls and he refused to accept them. Instead, they were sent back to Sutoku.

Sutoku was outraged by this rejection, and this was the final insult. In his rage, he bit off his tongue. As he bled to death, he pronounced a horrifying curse on the emperor and all of Japan. As he bled he transformed into a great tengu. His hair and nails grew long, and he never cut them again.

Eventually, Sutoku died. Caretakers set his body aside and awaited instructions from the emperor for the proper burial of Sutoku. After 20 days had passed, his body was as fresh as if he were still alive. Go-Shirakawa forbade anyone from mourning Sutoku, and there would be no funeral. The caretakers were taking his body to be cremated when a storm came in. They put Sutoku's body on the ground as they went for cover. As they approached his body, the stones around him were coated with fresh blood. After he was cremated, his ashes rose into the sky and formed a dark cloud which descended upon Kyoto.

For many years after this, Japan was wracked by disaster and calamity. Go-Shirakwa's successor, Emperor Nijo, died at the age of 23. All forms of disaster struck Japan. Storms, plagues, earthquakes, fires, and droughts gripped the nation. So many of Go-Shirakawa's supporters and allies died in battle that imperial Japan itself became weakened. By 1180, civil war had broken out. After five years, the imperial court was devastated. The Kamakura shogunate seized control of Japan. It is still believed that all this was the result of the curse of Sutoku.

These three Yokai are the evilest because the legacy they left was one of upheaval and near ruin. The order of society was ordained by the gods in the *Kojiki* and the *Nihon Shoki*. This order is a divine order and these evil Yokai were so powerful that they were able to upset or at least destabilize this order for many years.

Helpful Yokai

There are many more Yokai, and some are quite helpful. The Yokai are in many ways similar to the Irish Sighe, or little folk. They can be utterly evil and destructive. They can also be magical assistants to the daily struggles of the common people. As these tales developed and were passed down through that ages, it is easy to see how some of the Yokai came to be magical blessings in a rural life that could be harsh and difficult. Because the cycles of nature, the reality of disease, and the momentary caprice of fortune were utterly mysterious things to people the world over, the Japanese tradition created Yokai who could help explain these things.

Kudan

Kudan are examples of those Yokai who exist to bring good fortune or at least warn of dangerous events. Kudan are born from a cow and resemble calves with human faces. They can speak immediately. Kudan never live more than a few days. They offer prophecies and predictions. Kudan can predict great harvests or droughts. They do not determine the events, they simply predict them. As soon as a Kudan delivers its prophecy it dies. In this way, Kudan can at least offer people the chance to prepare in the event of something catastrophic.

Although certainly much older, reports of Kudan sprung up in great numbers at the end of the Edo period as the shogunate crumbles and Japan saw the return of imperial authority. It is believed that Kudan predicted Japan's wars of the 19th and 20th centuries. There was such faith in both the existence of Kudan and in their word that newspapers in Japan would claim the truth of their news by saying "as if a Kudan said." This phrase continues in the common language of Japan to this day.

The power and luck of Kudan are such that people are encouraged to wear talismans bearing the image of Kudan for good luck. Hawkers and sideshow men would make Kudan mummies from stillborn calves, and other animals stitched together and charge money for people to see them. People would pay a small amount to see the mummified Kudan in hopes they would get some of the luck and good fortune of the Kudan.

Amabie

Amabie, or more likely amabiko are similar to mermaids. They live in the sea and appear in a bright light. They are covered with scales, have a beaked face, and three legs.

Amabiko are similar to Kudan in that they often offer prophecies and predictions. Amabiko have the added benefit of providing protection from diseases. Amabiko seems to have begun making appearances around a time in history when diseases such as cholera were striking around the world. The amabiko arrived to offer protection.

Both the origin of the name amabie and the variations from amabiko are unknown. Some scholars believe the amabiko may actually be copied from other myths and legends from other parts of the world.

Japanese history actually records one sighting of an amabiko in 1846. In present-day Kumamoto several witnesses reported seeing a strange light out in the sea. Eventually, a government official went out to investigate. He claims to have encountered an amabiko who predicted a great harvest in the coming years. This amabiko further instructed him that in the event of an outbreak of disease, everyone should be shown a picture of the amabiko to ward off the disease. The harvest proved to be a tremendous crop. A picture of the amabiko was published in the local newspaper so everyone could see the picture in order protect them from disease.

Jinja hime

Jinja hime are in many ways more similar to the mermaids than the amabiko. They have the head and face of a human female. Their bodies are serpent-like with fins and scales. They live underwater and rarely interact with human beings. Jinja hime are servants of the Palace of the Sea King.

Beyond the differences in appearance, jinja hime are strikingly similar to amabiko. In fact, it is believed that jinja hime may be the source for the lore of the amabiko.

One story, similar to the one just mentioned, goes that a man encountered a strange mermaid-like creature in the sea. It approached him and predicted a great harvest in the coming years, but also an outbreak of cholera. The jinja hime also instructed the man to ensure that everyone be shown a picture of the jinja hime to protect them from the disease.

Kyorinrin

Kyorinrin is a spirit which assembles himself from books and scrolls which are left unread and unstudied. He is made of the pages and words from these neglected texts and creates long extendable arms from the pages of the books.

Kyorinrin adorns himself in ornate robes made from the scrolls which have been left neglected. He also builds a headdress from the scrolls which is adorned with tassels. With his long extendable arms, he attacks those who ignore the magnificent books. Kyorinrin berates them for their choice to remain ignorant.

Chapter 5 – Japanese Fairy Tales

Like the rest of the world, Japanese culture has a rich tradition of what we have come to know as fairy tales. These tales consist of those cautionary stories designed to scare children or teach them valuable lessons about the world. They are filled with strange magic and memorable characters who are wise and terrifying, amusing and silly, beautiful and grotesque. There are numerous collections of these tales. Illustrated versions are available. With the popularity of Japanese animation, many of these tales are available in comic book collections.

Many of these tales are quite old and existed in the oral tradition long before anyone wrote them down. Some tales appear to be for general amusement, and others carry lessons or morals.

Yet, as with fairy tales from around the world, the sheer enjoyment we can derive, young and old, from the fantastic stories of magic, strange creatures and monsters, and the unlikely events still entertain us even if we are not familiar with all the customs evoked throughout the tales.

My Lord Bag of Rice

Many years ago, lived a warrior who came to be known as Tawara Toda, which means "My Lord Bag of Rice." His real name was Fujiwra Hidesato. This is the story of how he came to be called Tawara Toda.

Since he was a warrior and it was not in his nature to sit back and do nothing. He decided one day to go in search of adventure. He strapped two swords on himself along with his bow. He then slung his quiver full of arrows over his shoulder and set out. It was not long or far before he came to the bridge at Seta-no-Karashi which stretches across the magnificent lake Biwa. As he walked across the bridge, he spotted a huge dragon. It appeared like a serpent, its body so huge it covered the entire width of the bridge. It looked as if the trunk of a tree covered the bridge itself. One of the dragon's enormous claws was perched atop the parapet at one end of the bridges while its tail rested on the other. It seemed to be sleeping, although as it breathed, fire and smoke shot out of its nose.

Hidesato was indeed shocked at the sight of the dragon. He did not exactly know how to proceed. As a brave warrior, he gave no thought of turning back. At the same time, to go forward certainly meant stepping on the dragon and risking his life. Hidesato saw no choice so onward he went. He could hear his footsteps as he stepped on the dragon's body and coils. Having made it across, he went on without giving it another thought.

As he walked on his way, he heard a voice call out. When Hidesato turned to look, he was surprised to see the dragon had disappeared. Instead, he saw an odd-looking man who was bowing his head toward the ground as if in ceremony. The man had bright red hair that ran over his shoulders and formed a crown over his head in the shape of a dragon's head. The man's clothes were sea-green and were covered with a patterns which resembled seashells. Hidesato knew this was not an ordinary man, and he immediately began to wonder what all this meant. How did the dragon disappear so quickly and without a sound, he wondered? Did the dragon turn into this man and what could that mean? With that, Hidesato approached the man and spoke: "Did you just call out to me?"

The strange man replied: "I did. I must ask something of you. Do you think you could help me?"

Hidesato spoke: "If I am able to do this, I will, but first, tell me who you are."

The strange man told him, "I am the Dragon King. My home is in this lake, and I live directly under the bridge."

Hidesato asked him to explain the task he required, and the Dragon King explained:

"I want you to kill my greatest enemy, the centipede, who lives just beyond here on the mountain." He continued:

"I have lived in this lake for many years; I now have many children and grandchildren. For years now, we have lived in terror because the monster-centipede comes down from the mountain, night after night, and steals off with a member of my family. If this continues for much longer, it will take all my children and will surely come for me. The situation is so dire I decided to ask the help of a human. For many days I waited on the bridge in the shape of the terrifying dragon. Everyone who approached ran away in horror. You are the first mortal who has been able to look at me and pass over without fear. Will you please help me destroy the centipede?"

Hidesato was moved by the story, and he promised the strange man that he would help him if he could. Hidesato asked the Dragon King where he could find the centipede. The Dragon King explained that it lived high atop Mount Mikami, but the centipede came to the lake every night at a specific time. It would be better to wait for it. So, the Dragon King invited Hidesato to his palace. As they descended into the lake, the water parted. Though he was conducted deep into the lake nothing even dampened him or his clothes. Hidesato had heard the stories of the sea king who lived in a magnificent palace, served by the fish of the sea. But nothing prepared Hidesato for the beauty of the Dragon King's palace. White marble walls made up the palace at the heart of Lake Biwa. There in attendance were all the fish of the lake. Goldfish, red carp, and silver trout made up the retinue of servants who attended the Dragon King and his guest.

Hidesato was amazed at the banquet which was laid before them. They were served crystalized lotus flowers. They ate with chopsticks made from ebony. As they ate, the sliding doors opened, and ten beautiful goldfish dancers entertained them. Ten red-carp musicians played the koto and the samisen. They forgot all about the centipede as the feast and the entertainment went on until midnight. The Dragon King was about to raise a glass of wine in honor of the warrior when they heard the thunderous footsteps of what sounded like an invading army.

Hidesato and the Dragon King ran to a balcony, and they could see far off, coming down a mountain, two glowing balls of fire. The Dragon King shook with fear.

The Dragon King cried out: "It is the centipede. It is coming for its prey. Now is the time to strike and kill it!"

Hidesato looked out at the sight; straining his eyes, he could see, just beyond the balls fire, the body of an enormous centipede. Its body wound down the mountain, and its many legs and feet glowed like lanterns in the sky.

Hidesato displayed no signs of fear. He attempted to calm the Dragon King. "Fear not. I will kill the centipede. Bring me my bow and quiver."

The Dragon King brought him his bow and quiver. Hidesato was surprised to see that he only had three arrows left in his quiver. Hidesato put an arrow in place and let it fly. To his shock, the arrow struck the centipede right between the eyes, but it bounced off its armored body without harming it. Undaunted, he fitted another arrow in place. This too he let fly. This struck the centipede in the center of its head, but this one also bounced off without harming the centipede. The centipede could not be hurt with weapons. The Dragon King saw this and became despondent.

Hidesato had one arrow left in his quiver. If he failed to stop the centipede with this arrow, it would surely make its way to the lake. It had wrapped its huge body around the mountain seven times. The light from its one hundred feet was reflected in the waters of the lake. It was getting close.

Hidesato thought for a moment and remembered that he has once heard that human saliva was deadly to centipedes. He worried, though, this was not an ordinary centipede. It was a monster that made him cringe at the sight of it. He knew this was his last chance. Taking the arrow out of the quiver, he put it in his mouth. He let the arrow fly.

The arrow struck the centipede in the middle of its head, and this time it punctured the skull right into the brain. The creature stopped still; it let out a horrifying shudder as the fire of its eyes dimmed. The one hundred feet also dimmed to darkness. As the light faded, the entire sky fell dark. Lightning flashed, and storm winds whipped as if the world itself was ending. The Dragon King and his children, all the servants, and all the entertainers cowered in fear as the palace itself shook. At last, the day dawned, and the centipede was gone from the mountain.

Hidesato hailed the Dragon King and invited him to come to the balcony and see for himself; the centipede was in fact dead. At this, all the inhabitants of the palace rejoiced. Hidesato pointed to the body of the centipede that was floating in the lake as it painted the waters red with its blood.

The Dragon King was so grateful that he could not contain himself. His entire family bowed before Hidesato and called him the bravest warrior in all Japan.

The King prepared another feast to thank the warrior. All kinds of fish was prepared: stewed, boiled, roasted, and raw. Dishes made from the finest coral and crystal were laid out for the feast. The Dragon King served the most exquisite wine Hidesato had ever tasted. That day, the sun shined on the kingdom, and the lake like it had never shined before.

The King did not want Hidesato to leave and tried to persuade him to stay. Hidesato told the king that he must leave. He had accomplished the adventures he had set out to find. The Dragon King and his family were sorry to see him go, and in their gratitude, the king and his family gave the departing warrior gifts for delivering them from the terrors of the centipede.

As Hidesato stood to leave, a line of servant fish appeared. Dressed in elegant ceremonial robes, they laid out the gifts from the Dragon King:

First, a bronze bell.

Second, a bag of rice.

Third, a roll of silk.

Fourth, a cooking pot.

Fifth, a bell.

At first, Hidesato tried to refuse the gifts politely, but the Dragon King insisted. Hidesato did not wish to offend the King's generosity and graciously accepted the gifts. An entourage of servants was appointed to transport the donations to Hidesato's home.

While he was gone, the servants of Hidesato's household wondered where he had gone. They were concerned but concluded that he must have been waylaid by the storm the previous night. When the servants saw Hidesato returning, they were amazed at the sight of the large procession which accompanied him. They announced to the household that he had returned. As soon as the Dragon King's men put down the gifts at Hidesato's step, they completely disappeared.

Hidesato recounted all that had happened to his household. They were amazed at the tale. As it turned out, all of the gifts from the Dragon King had magic power. Only the bell turned out to be ordinary, and Hidesato presented it to a nearby temple so that it could be rung at each hour of the day.

The bag of rice was inexhaustible. No matter how much the warrior and his family took out of the bag, it always remained full.

The roll of silk never ran out. Again, and again, they cut off pieces to make suits of clothes and always the roll of silk remained.

The cooking pot made the most sumptuous food. Everything cooked in it became delicious, and it cooked without the need of fire.

Hidesato became known throughout Japan. Because he never needed food, fire, or clothes, he eventually became very rich. Because of this he eventually became known as My Lord Bag of Rice.

The Story of Urashima Taro

In ancient times, in the province of Tango, there was a young fisherman who lived in the fishing village of Mizu-no-ye. His name was Urashima Taro. Urashima Taro was the son of a fisherman, and the skills he learned from his father had more than doubled in him. Urashima Taro was the most skilled fisherman in that part of Japan and could catch more Bonita and Tai in one day than the other fisherman could catch in a week.

Although he was highly regarded for his fishing skills, he was more well-known for his kind heart. He never hurt anyone or anything. No creature was too small for his kindness. Even when he was a boy, his friends would make fun of him because he would not join in when the other boys were teasing small animals. He wanted no part of this kind of cruelty.

One evening, as he made his way home from a day of fishing, he heard a great fuss from a crowd of children. He checked to see what the noise was about and discovered that a group of kids were tormenting a tortoise. One boy pulled the tortoise around. Another boy pulled the tortoise in the other direction. Another boy beat the animal with a stick while still another pelted it with a rock.

Urashima immediately felt pity for the tortoise and called out to the children:

"Stop tormenting that animal," he said. "If you keep it up, it will die!"

The boys did not care. They were at an age at which cruelty was all too common amongst boys. One of the older boys answered Urashima:

"Who care if it lives or dies. We don't care. We will do as we please."

And so, the boys went on with their torments of the tortoise. They were crueler than before. Urashima thought about how to deal the boys and decided that maybe he could convince them to give him the tortoise. He smiled at them and spoke:

You boys must be getting tired of this. Why don't you give me the tortoise? I would love to have it and take it home.

The boys refused and said: "Why should we give you the tortoise. We caught it, and it is ours."

Urashima replied: "Obviously, this true. You caught the tortoise, and I am not asking you to give it to me for free. I will buy the tortoise from you with money. What do you think about that?" Urashima held up a string that held several coins threaded through the center. He went on: "Look at these coins. You could buy anything you want with this money. It is worth much more than that old tortoise. Now be good sports and sell the tortoise to me."

The fact is, the boys were not bad after all. They were just mischievous boys, and soon Urashima won them over. His kind words and gentle smile persuaded them "to be of his spirit," as the Japanese expression goes. Eventually, the eldest boy offered up the tortoise.

"Alright then, Ojisan (which means "uncle"), you can have the tortoise if you hand over the money," said one of the boys. Urashima handed them the coins, and the boys gave him the tortoise. Excited with their newly acquired riches, they quickly ran off.

Urashima held the tortoise and spoke to it saying, "Poor thing, you are safe with me. I have heard that the stork lives for a thousand years, but the tortoise lives for ten thousand years. How close you came to having that long life cut far too short. If I had not been passing by, those boys would have surely killed you just for fun. Now I will take you to the sea so may find your way home. Be careful you do not get caught again. I may not be there to save you next time."

Urashima took the tortoise to the edge of the sea a released it. He watched as the creature slowly disappeared. As the sun was setting, he realized he was tired and went home.

The next day, Urashima was in his boat fishing as usual. It was a fine morning. The weather was perfect with a beautiful blue sky above. In the morning, he sailed into the sea. He threw his line into the water and continued passing the other fisherman as he drifted further out into the calm waters.

Urashima could not help reflecting on the tortoise from the day before. He wondered to himself, how nice it would be to live for thousands of years just like the tortoise.

As he was lost in his daydreams, he suddenly heard a voice call out his name, "Urashima, Urashima!" It was a soft and clear voice beckoning over the water. Urashima stood up to see who was calling his name and where the voice was coming from all the way out here in the sea. He could not see another boat anywhere he looked. There was no sign of another person anywhere. He appeared to be all alone.

This startled him at first. As he looked to the side of his boat, he spotted a tortoise. It was the same tortoise from the day before. Urashima spoke:

"Well, well, little tortoise. Was it you who just called out to me?"

The tortoise nodded his head and said:

"Indeed, it was I who spoke to you. Yesterday, o kage sama de (which means thanks to you, or, in your honorable shadow), my life was spared. I come to you now to thank you and to offer my gratitude for your kindness and generous spirit."

Urashima replied, "This is kind of you. Come up to my boat. I would offer you a smoke, but since you are tortoise, I am sure you do not smoke." Urashima laughed at this.

The tortoise laughed and said, "I would love some sake; it is my favorite, but you are right. I do not smoke."

Urashima then told the tortoise, "I do apologize. I have no sake with me but come onto my boat and dry yourself in the sun."

The tortoise climbed into the boat with a little help from Urashima. As he made himself comfortable in the warm sun, he asked Urashima:

"Urashima, have you ever seen the palace of Rin Gin, the Dragon King of the sea?"

Urashima replied:

"No, I have often heard of the Dragon King's realm under the sea, and though I have spent many years on the sea, I have never seen the palace of Rin Gin with my own eyes. It must be far away. I wonder if it exists at all."

"So, you have never been to the Sea King's Palace," said the tortoise. Then you have not seen one of the most magnificent sights in the universe. It is indeed far under the sea, but I know the way, and I can take you there. If you would like to see the Sea King's realm, I will guide you there."

To which Urashima said, "I would love to go there, and it is so kind of you to offer to guide me. But you must understand that I am a mortal man. I am not able to swim in the sea the way you can."

The tortoise stopped him and spoke, "Think nothing of this. You will not have to swim at all. You can ride on my back all the way there."

Urashima looked at the tortoise and saw his small size. He said, "How can it be possible for me to fit on your back? You are so small."

The tortoise simply explained, "Just give it a try, and you will see."

When the tortoise had spoken these last words, Urashima gave him a second look. The tortoise had grown large enough for a full-sized man to sit on his back. Urashima said to himself, "This is indeed strange, but all right…"

The tortoise behaved as if nothing was out of the ordinary and said, "Whenever you are ready, we will set off." With that, he leaped into the sea carrying Urashima on his back. Down they went, deeper and deeper into the sea. Not only did Urashima not grow tired, but he also did not even get wet from the sea. After a long journey, Urashima spotted in the distance, a magnificent gate. Behind the gate, he could see the rooftops of a breath-taking palace.

Urashima spoke with excitement, "This looks like the gate to some tremendous palace! Tortoise, what is this marvelous place?"

The tortoise answered, "That is the gate of the Rin Gin Palace. Beyond that, the large rooftop you see is the Palace of the Sea King himself."

"So, we have arrived at the Palace of the Sea King," said Urashima. He was utterly amazed.

The tortoise answered him, "We have arrived. That was fast, don't you think? You must kindly walk from this point."

The tortoise approached the gate and spoke to fish who was the gatekeeper:

"This is Urashima Taro from the country of Japan. I have brought him to the Palace of the Sea King as a guest. Will you kindly show him in?"

All the vassals of the king came out to greet Urashima. The red bream, the flounder, the sole, the cuttlefish, all offered courtly bows to the guest.

They bade him welcome and said, "Urashima Sama! Welcome to the Sea Palace, the home of the Dragon King of the Sea. You are most welcome! We are honored to have a guest from such a far-off country. And you, Mr. Tortoise, we are grateful to you for guiding Urashima here. Follow us and allow us to be your guides."

Urashima was just a poor fisherman. He did not know the proper way to behave in such a grand place. However, he felt welcome and at ease and followed his guides to the inner palace. When he reached the entryway, he was greeted by a princess. She was stunning, more beautiful than any human. Her dress was in a red and soft green color that reminded Urashima of the underside of a wave. Their golden threads were woven through her gown which shimmered as he looked. Her hair was black, and it streamed over her shoulders like a princess from ages ago. Her voice was like water music. Her beauty and majesty completely struck Urashima. In his amazement, Urashima almost forgot to bow to the lady, but as soon as he made ready to bow, she took him by the hand and led him to a place of honor at the upper end of the hall. She asked him to be seated.

The princess spoke: Urashima Taro, it is a great honor and pleasure to welcome you to my father's palace. Yesterday you saved the life of a tortoise. I was that very tortoise, and I have sent for you to thank you. If you like, you may live here forever, and I will be your bride. It is forever summer in this kingdom, and there is no sorrow here. You will live in eternal youth, and we will live in happiness forever!"

Urashima was amazed by her words and the sound of her voice. He was filled with wonder and joy, and he thought he had to be dreaming. At last, he answered:

"I thank you many times for your kindness. I would like nothing more than to stay in this magnificent place. Until today, I have only heard distant tales of this kingdom. I have no words for what I have seen here."

As he was speaking a great train of royal servants assembled. They were all dressed in the most exquisite ceremonial clothes and bearing great trays made of coral filled with the most delicious foods. Fish and seaweed, the kinds of things he had only dreamed of before. They laid all this out in front of the bride and bridegroom. Everything was celebrated with amazing splendor. The entire realm of the Sea King rejoiced. The pair made their vows three times with the wedding cup. Music began to play, and gold and silver fish came out of the waves and began to dance. Urashima had never known such happiness. Nothing in his life prepared him for the joy of this moment.

When everything settled down, the princess asked Urashima if he would like to walk around the palace and see all the kingdom. He followed the princess as she showed him around the palace. The walls were made of coral and inlaid with pearls. There were wonders everywhere he looked that exceeded his words. He could not even begin to describe what he saw. This was a kingdom of eternal youth and happiness.

Possibly most amazing to Urashima was the garden which displayed all four seasons at the same time. Winter, Spring, Summer, and Autumn could be seen all at once. In one direction he saw plum and cherry trees in Spring bloom. Butterflies flew from flower to flower while nightingales sang.

In another direction, he saw the lush green of Summer. He could hear cicada from the day and the cricket from the night.

Still, in another direction, Urashima saw the glorious leaves of Autumn. Magnificent Chrysanthemums were in bloom.

At last, he looked to the north where he saw the slivery snows of Winter. The trees and bamboo were covered with snow, and before his eyes, he could see a frozen pond.

Each passing day brought more wonders and dazzled him with happiness. After three days though, he began to remember who he was and where he was from. He started to remember all he left behind, his parents and his own country. He began to think he did not really belong in the kingdom of the Sea King. He finally said to himself:

"I do not think I can stay here. I have an old mother and an old father at home. What will become of them in my absence? They must be worried sick. I must go home before another day passes." With that, he hurriedly began to prepare himself to go home.

He then went to his beautiful wife, the Princess. He bowed low before her and spoke:

"Princess, I have been exceedingly happy here with you. You have been so kind to me. However, I have to say goodbye to you and return to my own country and my parents.

Princess Otohime began to weep. She spoke in a soft voice:

"I fear you are not happy here. Why else would you wish to leave me so soon? Why are you in such a hurry? Please stay one more day."

Even as she spoke, as beautiful as he found her plea, he remembered his parents. His duty to his parents was stronger than any pleasure or any love. He could not be moved. Urashima answered her:

"I am sorry, my Princess, 'I do not wish to leave you. You must not think that. It is that I must go to my parents. Just let me go for one day, and I promise I will return to you."

Though she was indeed sad, she said to him, "Then there is nothing I can do. I will let you go to your father and mother this very day. Instead of keeping you with me one more day, I will send you home for one day. First, let me give you this token of our love to take back with you." She gave him a beautiful lacquered box. It has a silk cord tied around it with tassels of red silk.

Urashima received the gift, but he had second thoughts about taking it. He said to the Princess, "It does not seem fitting that I should take still more gifts after all you have given me. But I do not wish to dishonor you, so I will take it." Then he thought for a moment and asked, "Please tell what is in the box."

The Princess answered him:

"It is the tamate-bako, the Box of the Jewel Hand. It contains something extremely valuable and precious. You must not open the box no matter what, or else something terrible will happen to you. Please promise me you will not open the box."

Urashima promised her he would not open the box. He then walked down to the shore where a large tortoise awaited him. Mounting the tortoise's back, he was carried away just as he had come. As he left, he looked back and bade farewell to Princess Otohime until he could no longer see her. Then he made ready to return home to his own country.

The tortoise carried him to the familiar shore, and Urashima stepped off. He watched as the tortoise swam away toward the Kingdom of the Sea King.

As Urashima looked around a strange feeling came over him. He looked at the people as they passed by, and he examined how they looked at him. He noticed how they stared at him so strangely. Everything looked the same, the shore and the mountains were familiar, but the people acted as if they did not recognize him, and he did not know any of the faces.

In his amazement he walked home to his parents he called out: "Father, Mother, I have returned!" Just then he saw a strange man come out of the house.

He thought to himself his parents must have moved while he was gone. He began to feel very nervous, and he did not know why.

Begging the strange man's pardon, Urashima asked him, "Until just a few days ago, I lived in this house. My name is Urashima Taro. Do you know where my parents have gone?"

The strange man looked very confused. He looked at Urashima and said:

"You are Urashima Taro?"

"I am he," said Urashima.

The man laughed and said, "You are not very good at telling jokes. There was a Urashima Taro who lived in this village, but that story is over three hundred years old. It is not possible that he is alive today."

Urashima heard this and was frozen with horror. He spoke again to the man:

Please believe me. I am Urashima Taro. I am astounded by this. I left this very spot no more than four or five days ago. Please tell me what I want to know!"

The man then grew serious: "Maybe you are Urashima Taro, but the Urashima Taro I know of lived three hundred years ago. Are you his spirit returned to visit the old home?"

Urashima became somewhat desperate. He said: "Of course I am not a spirit. I am alive before you. Look at my feet!" He stomped the ground to show the man because Japanese ghosts do not have feet.

The man replied, "All I know is that Urashima Taro lived three hundred years ago. You can read it yourself in the chronicles of the village.

Urashima was bowled over. He was filled with shock and horror. Even as he looked around, everything looked just a little bit different than he remembered. He came to the terrible realization that what the man told him was true. He felt as if he was in a dream. He started to realize the few days he had spent in the Palace of the Sea King had not been days at all. Each day must have been one hundred years. His parents had died many years ago while he was gone, and so had everyone he ever knew. They must have written down his story. He knew he could not stay and that he had to get back to his wife, the Princess, in the Palace of the Sea King.

He made his way back to the shore. In his hand, he held the box the Princess had given him. He did not know which way to go. He then remembered the box, the tamate-bako.

He remembered what the Princess had told him; that he was never to open the box because it contained something very precious and very dangerous. But he said to himself:

Even though he knew he was disobeying the Princess's one command, he still persuaded himself he was doing the right thing. Ever so slowly he loosened the silk and the red silk cords and opened the precious lacquer box. Out of the box came a little soft cloud and three wisps of cloud with it. For just a moment he covered his face. The cloud hung in the air for just a moment and then floated away over the sea.

Until that moment Urashima was young and filled with life. He was only 24 years old. But then, suddenly, his hair turned snowy white. His back bent over. His body withered, and he fell down dead on the shore of the sea.

Because of this simple act of disobedience, Urashima could never return to the Sea King's realm and join his Princess.

The elders who tell this tale explain to children to never be disobedient to those who are wiser. You may become withered like Urashima from a simple act of disobedience.

Chapter 6 – Folk Heroes and Heroines

The folk heroes and heroines of Japan are too numerous to name. They come from the ancient texts discussed at the beginning of this book and from various folk sources around Japan. Some of the figures persist in the imagination of the Japanese people to this day and have found new life in Manga and video games.

We will look at just two examples. It is important to note that some of the actions of these heroes may seem odd or unfamiliar to us because the virtues they embody are foreign to us today. Suffice to say that both of the examples below are revered national heroic symbols in Japan. They behave according to the honorable virtues of the home and the court. They are figures to be admired, and these storied remain a part of the Japanese imagination because the actions of these heroes are to be emulated.

The Tale of the Bamboo Cutter and Kaguya hime

Once, a long time ago, an old bamboo cutter named Taketori was out cutting bamboo, and as he cut open a shining stalk of bamboo, he discovered a small baby girl inside of it, no larger than his thumb. He and his wife were childless, so he decided to take her home where he and his wife would raise her as their own. They named her Kaguya hime, which means child of the supple bamboo.

As the child grew, he found that every time he would go to cut bamboo and cut open a shining stalk, he would find a small lump of gold. He and his wife soon became extremely rich. The child eventually grew to be a normal sized young woman, but she was extraordinarily beautiful. Taketori tried to keep everything secret, but eventually, word got around as to the stunning beauty of Kaguya hime.

In time, five princes arrived at the home of Taketori to ask him for his daughter's hand in marriage. They begged him until he finally relented and instructed Kaguya hime to choose one of the princes. Kaguya hime did not want to marry any of the princes and so, she assigned each one a task which she knew was impossible. She promised she would marry whichever prince managed to complete this task. For the first prince, she instructed him to bring her the stone begging bowl of the Buddha in India. She told the second to bring her a jeweled branch from the legendary island of Horai. The third she demanded the robe of the fire-rat of China. The fourth she sent to find a precious jewel from the neck of a dragon. The fifth she told to bring her a cowry shell-born of swallows.

The first prince knew the task was impossible and attempted to deceive Kaguya hime with a bowl that resembled the one she had asked for. She saw that it was fake and dismissed him. Two other princes tried to deceive Kaguya hime and were summarily dismissed. Another gave up after encountering tremendous difficulty. The last prince actually died attempting the task.

Eventually, The Emperor of Japan himself came to visit the strange beauty and, after seeing how beautiful she was, fell in love with her. He asked her to marry him. Because he was the Emperor, Kaguya hime did not demand a task from him. She simply told him she could not marry him because she was not from the world and would not be able to leave with him to the palace. He accepted this but continued to profess his love for her.

That summer, as Kaguya hime gazed at a full moon, her eyes filled with tears and she became inconsolable. Her elderly parents asked her why she was sad. She finally told them she was not from this world and that she must return to the moon, to her people. It is believed that the people of the moon sent her to earth to find care in a mortal couple in order to protect her from a great war in the heavens. The gold which Taketori had found all those years was payment from the people of the moon.

The Emperor, who was hopelessly in love with Kaguya hime, sent his guards to surround her so she could not be taken away. Soon the heavenly people of the moon came to retrieve her. The Emperor's guards were dazzled by the strange and bright light. As the people of the moon took her up, she wrote notes of apology and goodbye to her earth parents. She then took a small taste of the elixir of life and attached it to a letter to the Emperor. The people of the moon placed their robes on her, and she instantly forgot her life on earth and all of her sadness.

The parents of Kaguya hime were overwhelmed with sadness and took to their beds. The Emperor later read the note and he too was overcome with grief. He sent his guards out to the highest mountain with a letter to Kaguya hime and instructed that it be burned at the top of the mountain so she could read it. The Emperor did not wish to live forever, so he also instructed that the elixir of life be poured out at the top of the mountain. The guards carried out these commands, and at the top of Mount Fuji they burned the letter and poured out the elixir of life. That is how Mount Fuji came to get its name, which means "Mountain Abounding with Warriors.

Yamato Takeru

The legend of Yamato Takeru is taken from both the *Kojiki* and the *Nihon Shoki*. The importance of this great hero cannot be over-emphasized. He is regarded by some as a figure analogous to King Arthur in his heroism and stature.

It is believed by some that Yamato Takeru was a historical figure, the son of the 12th Emperor of Japan and that he lived sometime in the 4th century. Actual historians tend to doubt this. It is believed that historical "facts" from the *Kojiki* and the *Nihon Shoki* are at best a blend of fact and fiction designed to create a straight genealogical line from the gods to the actual historical Emperors.

The Legend of Yamato Takeru

Originally named Prince Yamato, Yamato Takeru killed his older brother. His grieving father was afraid of him from then on and banished him to Izumo Province, then to the land of Kumaso to fight of criminals and rebels.

Before leaving, Prince Yamato prayed at the shrine of Amaterasu, the Sun Goddess, and asked for her blessings. Since his aunt was a priestess of the Ise shrines, she presented him with a silk robe and told him it would work as good luck. He then departed with his wife and few loyal followers, for the Island of Kyushu to fight rebels and criminals.

The Emperor hoped that he would defeat the prince by sending him to a certain death, in fact, the prince proved himself a great warrior. He defeated all who resisted him.

One particular time, Prince Yamato dressed himself as a woman by wrapping the silk robe around him. He placed a comb in his hair and adorned himself with jewels. In this way, he was able to enter the tent of his enemies during a banquet. At one point, the leader of the band bid Yamato to serve him as a servant woman. In disguise, Yamato approached the man and killed both him and his brother. As the leader lay dying, he asked who the woman was who had destroyed him. As soon as he found out, he named the hero Yamato Takeru, which means The Bravest Yamato.

The King remained fearful of Yamato Takeru. He ordered him to go fight against the provinces in the east where there were people who disobeyed the imperial authority.

After defeating the rebels in the east, Yamato Takeru encountered an outlaw rebel named Idzumo. Yamato Takeru knew he had to outsmart the outlaw in order to beat him, so he befriended Idzumo for a time. Idzumo invited Yamato Takeru to go swimming. While Idzumo was in the water, Yamato replaced Idzumo's sword with a wooden sword. After they came out of the water, Yamato Takeru challenged him to a duel. Since Idzumo was armed only with a wooden sword, Yamato Takeru easily defeated him.

With this, he was welcomed at the imperial palace as a conqueror and a hero. The king threw a lavish feast in his honor.

Soon after this, Yamato was ordered to defeat another rebellion. This time the Emishi uprising in the east. Like before, he went to pray to the Sun Goddess. His aunt again gave him a magic gift. This time she gave him the great sword named Kusanagi no turugi which once belonged to the Gods. This is the sword discovered by Susano-o, the brother of the sun Goddess Amaterasu. This was the sword which Susano-o used to defeat the eight-headed serpent in ancient times. His aunt also gave him a bag of flints for striking fire.

While Yamato Takeru was in the province of Suruga, he was invited to go on a deer hunt. While out on the hunt, Yamato noticed flames surrounding him in the tall grass. A bushfire was approaching him, and flames and smoke were close to cutting off his route of escape. He then remembered the flints his aunt gave him, and he quickly struck them at the grass nearest him. At the same time, Yamato swung the great sword, Kusanagi and cut the high green blades of grass which cut a path for him to escape. At that moment, a great wind blew the flames away from him. Yamato realized that the Emishi tribesmen had trapped him. After he fled a near certain death, the sword was named the Grass Cleaving Sword.

Yamato Takeru then ventured further east after defeating the Emishi rebellion. He won many victories along the way. During one episode, his princess threw herself into the sea as a sacrifice to assuage the wrath of the Gods.

Yamato Takeru would go on to defeat a great serpent in the mountains which was terrorizing people and devouring them. He destroyed the serpent by twisting his arms around it. Though stung by the evil creature, he survived.

Prince Yamato Takeru also wrote the first renga poems revered in Japan. After all of his conquests, he died of a disease that is believed to be the result of a local god he had cursed in this youth. Upon his death, he was transformed into a white plover.

Prince Yamato Takeru is revered as a great hero in Japan to this very day.

Chapter 7 – Contemporary Versions of Japanese Mythology

Since so many of the myths and legends of Japan still resonate with the Japanese people, many of these ancient tales have found a new life in contemporary culture. Anime, Manga, and video games have made good use of the fantastic stories of Ancient Japan.

It should come as no surprise the myths and tales we have covered should be found in modern comics and cartoons. The fantastic, terrifying, and beautiful magic which attends so much of the lore of Japan makes an easy transition to animated tales of wonder. At the same time, since so much of this mythology is still a part of the modern imagination in Japan, the tales are easily identifiable for modern readers.

The *Kojiki* has been brought to life in the form of manga. There are versions which have fully animated the text and others which are more like graphic novels. The degree of faithfulness to the original varies as some authors and illustrators have been more interested in the terrifying battles and trips to hell than the spirituality found in the book. In any case, the *Kojiki* has been a fruitful source for many of the most popular animated versions of Japanese mythology. There are entire scholarly studies on this subject alone.

Yokai have provided the manga and video game industries with endless fodder for their monsters and heroes. Shuten Doji is brought back to life in a manga series in which he takes on the characteristics of a superhero, although his status as a demon and destroyer is never far away. The sheer number of manga series which co-opt the Yokai are too numerous to enumerate.

One important source for much of the contemporary re-telling of Japanese mythology and folklore is the collection of Yakushima tales. This collection brings together a number of myths and legends which sprung from an actual place in Japan. The island of Yakushima holds a legendary status in Japan. It is nearly a perfect circle at the southern end of the country. Filled with lush forests and hidden spaces, Yakushima is precisely the type of place we associate with magic and myth. Of all the tales which sprung from the Yakushima tales, undoubtedly the most famous is the story of Princess Mononoke. This story was adapted for a highly successful film produced by the nearly equally legendary Studio Ghibli and directed by Hayao Miyazaki in Japan. It was dubbed into English and enjoyed a successful run the world over. The origin of the tale lies in the Yakushima myths and legends.

The story of Princess Mononoke involves a battle between the forces of the newly emerging modern weapons and machines against the gods and enchantments of the forests of Yakushima. "Mononoke" is not a proper name but the name of forest spirits, the same spirits believed to inhabit Yakushima. As Prince Ashitaka learns to negotiate the different realms of the spirits and the humans who seek to utilize the resources of the forests, the conflict between these two realms intensifies.

The battles between the spirits, led by the great wolf goddess, and the humans who encroach upon the mystical forests is in many ways a tale of the clash between old and new Japan. As we saw in the earliest tales and myths of Japan, virtually everything in nature was animated and enchanted with some form of god or spirit. As Japan moved into the modern era, as the mechanization of its world took over these customs and beliefs, the powers of these myths lost their force.

With the contemporary versions of Japanese mythology, we see in films such as *Princess Mononoke*; we perhaps see the resurgence of the power of Japanese myth in contemporary Japanese culture. These myths and legend still carry a great deal of power in modern life, and the massive success of this film proves that fact.

Conclusion

The myths, legends, and folktales of Japan are numerous. Japan is an ancient culture and the mythological stories which date back to times before writing are murky and mysterious. Every region of Japan has its own myths and legends which animate sacred places and even individual homes. The Japanese tradition of worshiping ancestors offers a world of legend and myth itself.

Looking only at those ancient texts, the *Kojiki* and the *Nihon Shoki*, we can see that there is a world of things to study. The two books overlap in many ways, but each offers its own version. As with all texts that have come down through the ages as sacred, scholars have made much of even the smallest differences. Those who study and practice the Shinto religion which was eventually shaped by these ancient texts will find a reason to split hairs over the minute differences between the two books.

The Yokai are another topic of Japanese mythology which can be a lifetime study. There is such a wealth of varieties of Yokai. Some of the Yokai are specific to certain parts of Japan. These also have given scholars and interested readers and inexhaustible supply of things to explore.

We looked at the three most evil Yokai because these are viewed as having a pernicious influence on the history of Japan. Whether one sees these things as true or not, they are the mythological causes of a significant disruption in Japanese civil society. Shuten-doji seems to be the primary culprit for the crumbling of Imperial Japan.

Fairy tales are found the world over. Japan is no different on this account. Like the fairy tales we see in just about every part of the world, the fairies of Japanese mythology are hard to figure out. They are mischievous, helpful, evil, terrifying, beautiful—everything one would imagine about fairies. They play the same role in Japanese society as they do elsewhere. They offer cautionary tales as well as stories of wonder.

Finally, the Japanese value their heroes. There is a wealth of mythology in this realm as well. Just looking at Yamato Takeru, we can wonder how many versions of this story must be in circulation.

There is a resurgence of interest in the mythology and folklore of Japan. This swell of interest is obviously flourishing in Japan, but it has found an audience and readership around the globe. The old Yokai provide a wealth of material for manga and anime. There are now entire shelves of manga books available which make use of the Yokai legends. These spirits and demons are brought to life like never before with the talented illustrators and story-tellers who bring these books to the world. Again, the readership for these books is global. As it turns out, Japanese mythology strikes a chord with people around the world.

Anime and video games can bring the old legends to life in ways no one could imagine in times past. These media animate and re-imagine stories are from as far back as the *Kojiki*. The powers of those founding gods and goddesses can be brought to life and rendered in an interactive form in these new and emerging media.

Films such as *Princess Mononoke* have brought the mythology of ancient Japan to the world on a grand scale. The success of this film alone is unprecedented, and the entire source for this film comes from the magical and mythical island of Yakushima. We can provisionally draw two conclusions from the success of this film. The ancient myths and legends of Yakushima are alive and still carry tremendous force even for the modern imagination. And the mythology of Japan remains an inexhaustible realm even to this day. Our modern world, so dominated by technology, remains driven by the myths and legends of old. Underneath our sense of sophistication, we are still just as enchanted by gods and goddesses, serpents and wolves, magical creatures both evil and good—deep within us is the same sense of wonder at the world as those eyes and ears which recorded the *Kojiki*.

Part 3: Hindu Mythology

A Captivating Guide to Hindu Myths,
Hindu Gods, and Hindu Goddesses

Introduction: Understanding Hindu Mythology

At first glance, Hindu myth may seem confusing. Gods and men lose their heads (literally), appear by different names, and occasionally form rivers from watering pots—and that's just in one corner of the Puranas.

Keep in mind people have spent generations writing about and discussing these stories and beliefs; it's natural for your brain to hurt a little bit as you sort it all out. Just imagine you're at your boyfriend or girlfriend's family reunion trying to figure out how everyone's related. (Or not related, in some cases. Some people really do just show up for the pizza.)

Mists of History

The birth of Hinduism occurred, according to archeologists and anthropologists, in the Indus valley when two Indo-European tribes mingled their respective belief systems. The two tribes, the Aryans, and the Dravidians, combined their practices and pantheons, from which combination (over the course of several thousand years) emerged the Trimurti, the holy trinity of Hindu Gods. The Trimurti includes Brahma, the creator; Vishnu, the protector of the world; and Shiva, the maintainer, and destroyer. Other familiar gods from the Aryan culture (the nomads) include Indra, Soma, Agni, and Varuna. For the most part, these gods are still sought after and celebrated in the Hindu traditions today.

Modern Hinduism: Four Branches

The stories in Hindu myth stem from traditions within Hinduism, drawing on stories from ancient texts, like the Ramayana and the Mahabharata. The major traditions include Vaishnavism, Shaivism, Shaktism, and Smarta. Subtraditions include Nath, Lingayatism, Atimarga, Sauraism, and others.

Though the four major traditions might share ceremonies or even beliefs, Vaishnavism, Shaivism, Shaktism, and Smarta each propound their own practices and philosophies.

Vaishnavism or *Vishnuisim* believes Vishnu is the supreme manifestation of God. Other gods and demigods—like Rama and Krishna—are, in fact, visualizations of Vishnu and his greatness. The followers of this sect, called Vaishnavas, are non-ascetic, meaning they're not interested in extremely simple lifestyles. i.e., sackcloth and ashes (in the Christian tradition) or other forms of self-denial for the sake of enlightenment.

Shaivism, considered the largest contingent within the Hindu tradition, believes Shiva is the supreme manifestation of God. Shaivites or Saivites spread to Southeast Asia, building temples and spreading their taste for yoga and the ascetic life with them. In some areas, Shaivism and Buddhism evolved together; some Shaivist temples feature Buddhist symbols and carvings.

Shaktism, closely related to Shaivism, believes "The Goddess" is the supreme manifestation of God. "The Goddess" is the divine feminine, worshipped in the form of Devi or Shakti. Devi is a partner with Shiva.

Smarta believes in Panchatayana puja, or equal worship for five main gods and goddesses: Shiva, Vishnu, Surya, Devi, and Ganesha.

If you want to keep the different contingents straight, remember:

Vaishnaivism=Vishnu
Shaivism=Shiva
Shaktism "shakes it up" with Shakti. Belief in the divine feminine.
Smarta=5 letters in "smart" for 5 different gods

Holy Texts: Shruti and Smrti

The stories from Hindu myth originate from two different books of scripture—the shruti and smrti.

Shruti, meaning "that which is heard" forms the backbone of Hindu philosophy. The Vedas, the Brahmanas, and the Upanishad fall into this category. The Shruti are considered authorless and ageless.

Smrti, meaning "that which is remembered" includes the Puranas and the Epics, like the Ramayana and Mahabharata. The Smrti are attributed to an author. The Bhagavad Gita is part of the Mahabharata.

Philosophy

The Hindu philosophical traditions include the Sankhya, Yoga, Nyaya, Vaisheshika, Mimamsa, and Vedanta. These—the Astika, or orthodox—accept the Vedas as authoritative. The Nastika—the unorthodox—reject the Vedas and include Buddhism, Jainism, Carvaka, and Ajivika.

The Astika philosophies are traced through the Vedas and other Hindu scriptures, popping up alongside mythological facts and figures. They shape the perspective in the stories and make up the ontological bones.

Myths and Legends

Why does any of this background matter?

The myths you're about to read are steeped in these foundations. These stories—Ravana the rakshasa and his ten heads, Lord Ganesha and his mouse mount, the protection of Krishna—are really about the people who tell them and the meaning they try to make of them. A basic understanding of the roots of Hinduism can help you to find the golden threads among an intricate tapestry of heritage and belief. The symbols of these myths—lotus flowers, multiple heads or arms, tapasyas—richly represent thousands of years of perspective and worship.

Keep in mind that because different versions of Hinduism inspire different people, many different versions of the stories float through the jungle and over the stones of temples and traditions. The stories in this volume are my version, though I've stuck as closely to the original myths and legends as imagination allows. At the end of this book, you'll find a short bibliography for further research and reading.

Namaste.

Chapter 1: Lord Brahma, Lord Vishnu, and the Beginning of the World

In the beginning, there was only nothingness and the Brahman. (Not to be confused with Brahma—he came later.) The Brahman—formless and beyond description—drew out the nothingness and created beings, glorious immortals steeped in the power and lifeblood of eternity.

From its conceptual self, the Brahman created all things, starting with Lord Brahma and Lord Vishnu. Thus, were formed two of the three greatest gods. Though other immortals came after, these were the mightiest and most honored.

Vishnu napped on the water, the first object created. The cool waves lulled him to sleep, rocking his greatness on their crests. His skin was blue.

A shining egg appeared in the water, glowing as brightly as the sun. Brahma formed himself within the egg, growing and molding his form for a thousand years. Eventually, Brahma burst from the egg. The two pieces fell apart, creating heaven and earth, respectively. Hidden inside those pieces were the landmasses. Brahma shaped them with his mighty hands, forming the continents from the water.

After he shaped the world, Brahma meditated. From his elevated thoughts sprang ten sons. (Gods aren't always born the same way as men.) These were the sages, the founts of wisdom to whom Brahma revealed his wisdom. Another god, Dharma, emerged from Brahma's mighty chest.

Others tell another story. Lord Vishnu, the protector, and preserver, formed for himself a Chaturbhuj, a form with four arms. Prakriti, the feminine creative force, joined him in his effort. In his arms, he held a lotus flower and his mace, the weapon of justice. From the ocean's waves came Lakshmi, whom Lord Vishnu accepted as his consort.

From his navel grew a lotus flower, and its blossom stretched across the ocean. From the blossom emerged Brahma, the creator, and friend to Vishnu throughout eternity.

Thus began the world of the gods, the dawn of the first beginning.

Chapter 2: The Birth of Lord Shiva

A short time after the creation, Lord Brahma and Lord Vishnu chanced upon each other while walking in an empty plain.

"Greetings, Lord Brahma," said Lord Vishnu, respectfully.

"Greetings, Lord Vishnu," Brahma responded. "Where are you going over this barren plain?"

"I go to look over my greatness," said Lord Vishnu, proudly. "In this world, my devotion takes first importance, and I go to listen to the prayers of my people."

This reply did not please Lord Brahma.

"Many may pray to you, Lord Vishnu," he said, "but they forget whom it was who gave them lips to pray. When they honor you in prayer, they honor me more, since I gave them the ground on which to worship."

Lord Vishnu scowled, and the ground beneath him shook.

"If there be a greater power than I, then let him manifest!"

Between the two gods appeared a blazing pillar that stretched both into the sky and into the depths of the earth. Its light blinded them, and they raised their hands to ward off the glare. They craned their necks back until they touched the earth, yet they could not see the end of the pillar.

Lord Brahma and Lord Vishnu were filled with wonder. Who could be mightier than both the Creator and the Preserver of the world? They decided to seek the end of the pillar.

"I shall change into a goose and seek the end of the pillar in eternity," said Lord Brahma. He stretched out his arms, and they grew great white feathers, and his face narrowed to a goose's thin bill.

"I shall change into a boar and seek the end of the pillar in the earth," said Lord Vishnu. His blue skin changed to matted hair, and his nose grew long, sharp tusks.

Lord Brahma leaped into the sky and Lord Vishnu dove into the earth, both seeking the end of the great pillar without a name.

Lord Brahma beat his wings and soared past the treetops. He beat them again and rose above the hills. He beat them again and floated above the mountains. The pillar stretched higher still. He beat his wings even higher and soared among the heavens. He beat them again and rose among the stars. The pillar stretched higher still. Lord Brahma flew for ages, beyond time and eternity itself, until his wings ached and his feathers drooped with fatigue. Still there was no end to the pillar. He returned to the empty plain.

Lord Vishnu dug deep into the earth, past the roots of plants and trees. He dug further, snuffling his nose deeper, past the roots of rivers. The pillar stretched deeper. He dug deeper, past the feet of mountains. He dug deeper and deeper into the bottom of the earth itself. The pillar stretched farther still. Lord Vishnu dug until his tusks were dulled and his whiskers drooped with fatigue. Still there was no end to the pillar. He returned to the empty plain.

"Lord Brahma!" called Lord Vishnu, when he saw Lord Brahma land on the grasses. "I have dug and dug and cannot find the end of the pillar. It does not end in the earth."

"Ah, Lord Vishnu!" returned Lord Brahma. "I have flown and flown and cannot find the end of the pillar. It does not end in the sky."

The pillar shook, and the earth trembled. It shook again, and the sky shuddered. It shook a third time, and a shining figure stepped from its depths.

His skin was marred with bhasma (ashes), and his head was matted and curly. A third eye called Tryambakam burned in his forehead. A snake hissed at his throat.

He lowered his trident, the trisul. Lord Brahma and Lord Vishnu bowed in acknowledgment. Here truly was a power as great—if not greater—than their own.

Thus was born Lord Shiva, the destroyer, Lord of demons. He made his home in Varanasi, and married Parvati, from whom he was rarely separated. But that is a story for another page.

Chapter 3: Saraswati & Brahma's Fifth Head

After the creation, Brahma looked over the world and was pleased. He saw the water and land, the mountains and hills. He saw the sun, Aditya, whose rays blessed the earth. He saw the sages, sprung from his thought. But none of these beings, as yet, had been born to a mother and father.

So, Lord Brahma drew from his own body a form, half male and half female. The male was called Swayambhu Manu, and the female Shatarupa. We know her better by another name: Saraswati.

Saraswati's dark hair stretched to her waist, and her face was pure and open. In her hands, she held a veena by which to bless the universe with music and wisdom. Hansa, the swan, bore her on his back.

When he saw the beauty of Saraswati, Lord Brahma's soul moved within him. He longed for her as his wife. But Saraswati, drawn from his own body, was like his daughter.

One day she approached Lord Brahma to pay her respects. He gazed at her with intense desire. When she circled behind him, he could see her no longer. So great was his longing that a second head sprouted from behind his first one, the better to gaze on Saraswati and her beauty.

Saraswati passed to Lord Brahma's left, and a third head appeared to gaze at her still. When she passed to his right, yet another—a fourth head—sprouted from his shoulders so she could not escape his sight.

The attention troubled Saraswati. To gain a moment's peace from Brahma's desire, she jumped over his head. A fifth head sprouted from Brahma's shoulders so that Saraswati could find no rest from his interest.

Lord Shiva witnessed the performance and was displeased.

"It is not lawful to pursue your daughter, Lord Brahma," he said. Four of Brahma's heads praised Shiva in agreement. The fifth head hissed and reviled Shiva for his interference. Lord Shiva drew his sword.

"A head that speaks in such a way shall not speak at all."

And so Lord Brahma lost his fifth head that spoke evilly to Lord Shiva. Eventually, Brahma and Saraswati married, and have lived together since. Shatarupa married Swayambhu Manu and produced the first children. Thus began the cycle of fathers and mothers from the first man and woman.

Chapter 4: Shiva Tests Parvati

In the Himalayas there lived a great king. He and his wife, Mena Devi, served Lord Shiva and offered him many respects. But they were unfulfilled. They wished for one thing and one thing only: for a daughter to grow and become the wife of Shiva.

"Oh, that our family could be worthy of this honor!" cried Himavantha, the king. "I am a ruler, yet I am poor as the poorest peasant without this gift."

"Then let us perform a tapasya," answered Mena Devi. "It will please Gauridevi, the wife of Shiva. Perhaps she will be reborn as our daughter."

King Himavantha agreed. Mena Devi began her tapasya. The sun rose and fell, and still, she meditated. The shadows chased themselves across her face, and still she meditated. No food crossed her lips, and no water wet her tongue. Finally, after three days, Guaridevi heard the meditation of Mena Devi.

"I am pleased by your devotion," said Guaridevi. "What do you ask of me?"

"Great goddess," said Mena Devi, bowing herself to the ground. "Himavantha is a great ruler among men, and I am his wife. But our wealth is nothing without a blessing. We wish only to have you as our daughter, and raise you to be the wife of Shiva."

The request pleased Guaridevi.

"I will be reborn as your daughter. Lord Shiva will grieve, but he will find me again."

Guaridevi leaped into a fire. Her form as Gauridevi perished in the flames, and Shiva lamented her loss. Meanwhile, Mena Devi conceived and bore a daughter; she named her Parvati. Her first word was Shiva, and by this, her parents knew that Gauridevi had kept her promise. Parvati grew fairer and wiser every day until she was finally of the age to seek Shiva.

After Guaridevi perished in the flames, Lord Shiva meditated for many years to mourn her loss. He meditated so deeply that he neither heard sound nor saw sights without the depth of his mourning. When the time came for Parvati to wed Shiva, he could neither see nor hear her. The king consulted with Narada, a wise sage.

"What is to be done?" King Himavantha asked. "Our daughter must wed Lord Shiva, but his mind wanders in other paths."

"Lord Shiva is deep in meditation," answered Narada, "but the prayers of worship may still reach his ears. Send Parvati to pray at his shrine, and perhaps he will hear her voice if her devotion is pure."

Himavantha was pleased with this counsel and sent Parvati to the shrine of Lord Shiva. When Parvati's eyes fell on Lord Shiva deep in his mediation, her heart danced within her, and she determined to offer reverence to none but him. She performed tapasya in his honor and offered him worship by every means within her power. Her devotions did not cease with the night but continued through till the dawn. She prayed until her voice croaked and her eyes drooped with fatigue. Deep in his meditation, Lord Shiva heard her prayers.

"This truly is a pure woman," he thought, "who prays and offers worship to me without ceasing. Perhaps I shall take her as my wife."

But first Lord Shiva sought to test Parvati, for perhaps she loved something better than he. He dressed in robes of gold silk and wore the face of a rich Brahmin. Coming to the shrine where Parvati continued to pray, he feigned oblation to Shiva before turning to her.

"Would you waste your devotions at a shrine of no consequence?"

Parvati's eyes flashed, but she did not stop her worship. Lord Shiva hid his smile and tried again.

"Would you wish to live without wealth, with only the ashes as your comfort?"

Parvati turned her back to him and continued to pray, but her hands shook with anger. Lord Shiva was pleased but tested her a third time.

"It would be a pity for a beautiful, rich girl to marry a poor beggar, though he be a god."

Parvati spun around.

"I will marry none but Shiva!"

"I am he."

Lord Shiva cast away his disguise, revealing his true nature. Parvati clapped her hands for joy and fell at his feet. Lord Shiva raised her gently.

"You have proven your devotion. I will take you as my bride."

Himavantha and Mena Devi were overjoyed by Parvati's marriage and blessed the goddess for keeping her promise to them. And so, Lord Shiva and his consort, Parvati were married.

Chapter 5: Shiva Snares a Whale

Lord Shiva undertook to teach his wife Parvati, about the Vedas. They sat down in the garden behind their home, where the flowers bloomed, and the grasses waived in the mountain breeze.

"Listen, Parvati, to the beauty of the Vedas and the wisdom therein," said Lord Shiva. Then he began. He unfolded the gyan, the knowledge, and Parvati listened. The day stretched into a week. He bathed his understanding in the Rig Veda, the Sama Veda, the Yajur Veda, and the Atharva Veda. The week stretched into months. Lord Shiva examined the Samhitas, speaking their mantras and singing their prayers. He revealed the Aranyakas and explained the rituals and ceremonies. The months stretched into years. He reviewed the Brahmanas and their commentaries and meditated over the Upanishads. The years stretched into a thousand years, and the seasons swelled and faded around them like the heartbeat of the earth. Still, Lord Shiva expounded the Vedas and their wisdom and delighted in their words.

Parvati listened. She listened to the mandalas and the meters of the hymns and hummed quietly with them. She listened as the trees stretched their roots deeper into the mountain soil and birds sang their lives away. After many years, her eyes drooped with fatigue, and she yawned.

Lord Shiva frowned. "Have you lost your interest, Parvati?"

"Only for a moment," she replied. "My eyes drooped with fatigue and I yawned without taking thought. I am listening now."

Lord Shiva was displeased.

"Go to earth and take birth as a fisherwoman."

"What have I done to deserve punishment?" Parvati cried.

But Lord Shiva did not reply. He stalked away, and the ash flaked from his skin and the skulls around his neck clicked and clacked in ire. Parvati obeyed. She took the form of a beautiful baby girl, who cried and cried until a fisherman noticed her kicking under a tree. He picked her up and carried her home, for his wife had died, leaving him no children, and he was glad to find one to be his own.

Lord Shiva climbed to the top of his mountain to meditate. He meditated for many years, but when he came to himself again, Parvati was still absent. He traveled to the four mountain faces, and in the glitter of crystal, ruby, gold, and lapis lazuli he saw the beauty of Parvati and her love for him. His heart was heavy then, and he regretted his punishment.

Parvati grew more beautiful every day. She learned to row, and soon rowed the fastest of any other in the village. She learned to fish and assisted her father with his catch. Soon he became the wealthiest man in the village.

Lord Shiva sat by himself on Mount Kailasha. The air was empty without the sound of Parvati's voice; his home was empty without her presence. Lord Shiva sat sadly until his shoulders drooped and his matted hair dragged in the dirt. Nandi, the wise bull upon which Shiva sometimes traveled, saw his master's grief.

"Can you not call Parvati back?" he asked. "I know she would come if you asked her."

"I cannot," said Lord Shiva, and great tears rolled from all three of his eyes. "Parvati's destiny requires her to marry an angler."

And he sighed such a great sigh that the clouds around Mount Kailasha tossed and heaved like a summer storm. Nandi sorrowed when he saw Lord Shiva aching for his wife.

"What can I do to help Lord Shiva?" he wondered. "I must find a way to ease his sadness."

Nandi went to Parvati's village and watched while she rowed and fished with her father. She laughed as the water splashed over the side of the boat and sang with the whisper of the waves.

"Her voice ought to be on Mount Kailasha, not here in a fisher village," thought Nandi. "But since she cannot yet return, perhaps my master can meet her here."

Nandi changed himself into a great whale. His body stretched longer than four fisher boats and his tail gleamed like a waning half-moon. He waited until the fishermen pushed out to the fishing grounds, and then followed their boats stealthily. When they cast their nets to fish, Nandi tangled them in his fins and tore them from the boats. The fishermen lamented their bad luck and cast out new nets. Again, Nandi tangled their nets in his fins and tore them off. The fishermen poked at him with their oars, and he flipped over their boats. Finally, the fishermen gave up and headed back to shore without their catch.

For the next several days Nandi plagued the fishermen. He tangled their nets and tipped their boats. He scared away the fish and made great, rough waves with his tail. Day after day the fishermen went home with empty nets and stomachs. Eventually, their complaints reached the ears of Parvati's father, who was a wealthy leader among them. He listened while they spun the tale of the trickster whale that spoiled their fishing, and then raised his hands for silence.

"He who catches the whale," he said, "will have my daughter as a wife. He must not plague our village anymore."

The fishermen murmured in excitement and set straightaway for their boats. They baited their lines with tasty morsels and stretched large nets between spaces in the rocks. They roamed among the waves, poking the crests with their spears. But none could catch Nandi. He stole their bait, stretched and broke the nets, and escaped the points of the spears. One by one the fishermen turned back. None could catch the whale.

Parvati's father worried for the village if they could procure no food. He prayed to Lord Shiva day and night. Parvati stood by him in his vigil and offered him water when his lips went dry.

"Please Lord, help to rid us of this crafty whale."

He prayed until his eyes drooped with fatigue. Finally, when he could pray no longer, Parvati whispered for him.

"Please, Lord Shiva, hear my father's prayer."

Far away on the top of Mount Kailasha, Shiva heard Parvati's words. They floated on the wind and settled into his heart, and he received them gladly. He transformed himself into a young man and presented himself before Parvati's father.

"I will catch this whale," he said, "and earn the hand of the maiden."

Parvati blushed but smiled at the handsome stranger. Lord Shiva boarded his boat and paddled out to the fishing grounds. Nandi heard the voice of his master and swam nearby. When Lord Shiva cast out his line, Nandi leaped for the hook. When Lord Shiva showed the fisherman that he had caught Nandi, the whale, he was given Parvati to wife.

Thus were Lord Shiva and Parvati reunited and Nandi the whale tamed.

Chapter 6: Ganesha Loses His Head

At times Lord Shiva is absentminded. It is a great responsibility to meditate and to chase the negative forces from the world; so great, perhaps, that other obligations is swallowed up in the way.

One day, Lord Shiva approached the hour of his departure. He hugged and kissed his wife fondly.

"I will return shortly," said he, "once the negative forces have been expelled."

Parvati embraced him and wished him good fortune.

"May you find success in your journey and return home without incident."

Lord Shiva went away to meditate. The negative forces were significant at that time, and it required much focus and effort to cast them away.

Parvati waited patiently, but her husband did not return. Soon she began to be big with child. Still, she waited for her husband. When the child was born, she named him Ganesha. He and his sister, Ashoka Sundari, filled Parvati's days with laughter and sunshine and eased the ache of Shiva's absence. Ganesha grew into a healthy boy and helped his mother and sister greatly.

After some years, Lord Shiva shook himself from deep meditation and found that he missed his wife. The negative forces had been dispelled, and he was free to return home. He made the journey as quickly as he could and was surprised to find a man-child standing by the gate. Lord Shiva made to enter the house, and the man-child stopped him.

"You shall not enter into this house," said Ganesha, for he did not recognize his father, who had been absent for so many years. "The goddess is not prepared to receive you."

Lord Shiva smiled and made to brush the boy aside. Ganesha resisted and blocked the way.

"You shall not enter," he repeated. He stood in front of the gate and folded his arms.

Lord Shiva frowned. He did not know that he had left Parvati pregnant with this son.

"How is it that I cannot enter at my own home?" he said. "Move aside, child."

"This is my home, and I do not know you," said Ganesha defiantly, "so you shall not pass."

Lord Shiva was displeased and impatient to see his wife. Without another word, he sliced the head from Ganesha's shoulders and tossed the body to one side. He met Parvati coming from a bath and opened his arms to embrace her. But the body of Ganesha peeped out from the corner of the house, and she fell to her knees, wailing.

"Ah, my son! My Lord, what has happened? My son, my son!"

"Your son?" Lord Shiva said, astonished.

"Our son," replied the goddess, as she cradled Ganesha's body in her arms.

"I knew him not when I arrived," said Lord Shiva, and he told Parvati all he had done. Parvati wept bitterly, and her tears watered the ground. Ganesha's sister wept also as she hid behind a bag of salt. Ever after Asohoka Sundari was linked with the taste of salt, because of her fear of her father and her grief for her brother. To comfort Parvati, Lord Shiva proposed a solution.

"Because he is our son, I may seek for him a new head to put on his shoulders and replace the old one. I will take the head from the first being I find asleep and bring it back from our son, who shall be whole again."

And so Lord Shiva left and searched for a new head for Ganesha. He searched in the river, and he searched in the mountain but found no new head for his son among the water and rocks. He searched further still in the jungle below and found a baby elephant sleeping. Lord Shiva plucked off its head and carried it back for Ganesha.

When Parvati saw the heavy elephant head on her little son's shoulders, she cried and cried, but there was nothing more she could do. Lord Brahma and Lord Vishnu blessed the boy and sealed Lord Shiva's gift.

Thus, ever after Ganesha bore the head of an elephant.

Chapter 7: Ganesha Spills a River

Many years ago, Sage Agastya lived in a dry and barren country. The plants wilted, and the cracked earth ached for water. Sage Agastya withdrew himself to a sacred place and prayed mightily to Lord Brahma and Lord Shiva.

"Oh great Lords who offer blessings of peace and cultivation," he said. "Hear the prayers of your humble servant and bless this broken land that your names may be reverenced forever."

The gods heard his prayers. Lord Brahma and Lord Shiva appeared to Sage Agastya.

"What will you?" asked Lord Shiva. The skulls around his neck clicked and clacked together, but Sage Agastya did not fear. He bowed his head.

"Great Lord, give me sacred water to bless this land, that the plants and people may grow strong and well-formed."

"It shall be done," Shiva replied. "Bring forth your kamandalu, and I shall fill it."

Sage Agastya brought forth his little water pot and offered reverence to Lord Brahma and Lord Shiva. Lord Shiva poured into the kamandalu the purest of liquid, the sacred water necessary to start a river. Sage Agastya thanked Lord Shiva and carried the kamandalu away.

He traveled many days over the land, seeking the best place to start the new river. Some hills were too high. Some valleys were too low. Finally, he made his way to the Coorg Mountains. Their green heads brushed the clouds. He sat down on a rock to rest, cradling the kamandalu filled with sacred water in his arms. After a short time, a small boy came down the path.

"Young child," called Sage Agastya. "Will you hold my kamandalu while I relieve myself?"

"Yes, Sage Agastya," said the boy, smiling. "I will hold it."

"Take care," said the sage. "It is filled with sacred water, and it is dangerous to spill."

"I will take care, Sage Agastya."

Sage Agastya gave the boy the kamandalu and went away directly to relieve himself. Once he was gone, the boy laughed and set the kamandalu on the ground. The boy was Ganesha, son of Lord Shiva, and he thought that valley perfect for a new river. The water would spill down from the high places and wash the feet of the mountains below.

When Sage Agastya returned, he was annoyed to see the boy sitting on the rock and the kamandalu sitting on the ground.

"You have neglected the sacred water!" he scolded. "Look, here comes a crow to sully it with his beak. Shoo!"

But the crow did not fly away. He looked at Sage Agastya, and then bent his beak to take some water. Sage Agastya beat the air with his arms, scaring the crow away. The crow's claws caught the edge of the kamandalu, spilling the sacred water. Immediately a river sprang up and rushed down the mountainside.

 Thus was born the River Kaveri, the sacred river prayed for by Sage Agastya, gifted by Lord Shiva, planned by Ganesha, and spilled by a crow.

Chapter 8: Kubera's Pride

On an important festival day Kubera, Lord of the Yakshas, held a feast. His host delivered silk napkins to every guest. The servers carried fine toasted fish and biryani, and chahou kheer porridge steamed in golden bowls. Prestigious guests crossed the threshold. Varuna arrived with his consort Varuni, and her hair glittered with sparkling seashells. Tvastr, the heavenly builder, bowed to Indra, the king of the gods. Though Lord Shiva and Parvati could not attend, they sent their son, Ganesha, as their representative. It was a feast of decadence, and Kubera soaked in the glory of his wealth.

The guests sat down to eat, and all were pleased with the spread. Varuna praised the amritsari fish while Varuni tasted sweet imarti. Tvastr supped savory dal, and dum aloo and Indra relished milky shahi paneer. Their cups were full, and the guests laughed and joked on plush rugs and pillows.

Lord Ganesha consumed the rajma beans and naan bread. He devoured samosa and tandoori chicken. He demolished balls of pani puri and pots of palak paneer. The decadent feast disappeared, one golden platter at a time. The other guests halted their discussion and watched as each dish slipped down Ganesha's empty throat. He devoured the dishes, the napkins, and the tablecloth. He swallowed the candles, the singers and dancers, and even the tables and seats; the host's flailing arms and gold-shod feet slipped away as Ganesha swallowed him whole.

"Please, Great One!" Kubera cried again. "Spare my people!"

But instead, Ganesha swallowed the plump pillows and ornate tapestries. He swallowed the candles and the kamandalu, and the water sloshed in his great stomach.

"Stop, Lord Ganesha!" cried Kubera horrified. "Let your hunger be appeased!"

But Lord Ganesha did not stop. He swallowed and swallowed until all of Alakapuri, the city of Kubera, trembled in terror. Kubera placed his swiftest shoes on his feet and ran to Lord Shiva's home on Mount Kailash. He sprinted past the rivers feeding the grass as they wound on their way. He ran past the hills where the cattle and elephants grazed. He ran to the mountains where the birds sang sweetly and fed upon the rich fruit and berries.

Finally, he arrived at the home of Lord Shiva, where the great lord and his consort, Parvati, sat eating a simple meal.

"Lord Shiva! Hear my pleadings and cause Ganesha to cease devouring," Kubera said, falling at Lord Shiva's feet. "My city shakes, and my people tremble in fear because of his ceaseless hunger."

Lord Shiva said nothing but smiled a little as he stood. From his table he lifted a cup of plain, roasted grains, and carried it back to Alakapuri, walking calmly the whole way. Kubera followed, wondering perhaps if it had been a mistake to consult Lord Shiva after all.

When they arrived, Ganesha had torn the doors off their hinges and swallowed them whole. Lord Shiva handed Ganesha the cup of roasted grains.

"Ah," sighed Ganesha, restfully. "I am appeased."

Ganesha's hunger for food ceased, and he sat quietly on the bare ground. Kubera bowed his head in shame.

"Forgive my weakness, Lord Shiva. I saw only my wealth and not the good purposes for which it might be used. In my eyes, the gold of plate and fork glittered more brightly than the eyes of my people. I am reproved."

Thus, Ganesha consumed the sumptuous feast, and Kubera learned his prideful mistake.

Chapter 9: Ganesha Injures a Goddess

Once, when Lord Ganesha was in his infancy, he found a shabby housecat in a village near his home. The cat curled under a set of worn wooden stairs, and dust marred her coat.

"Come play with me!" Little Lord Ganesha commanded the cat. It slunk further into the shadows and hid its eyes with its striped tail. Lord Ganesha was displeased and pulled the cat out from under the porch by her hind leg. He swung her into the air and caught her again, and then threw her high in the air to see how many times she could land on her feet. The poor cat was soon tired and covered in bruises. Lord Ganesha tired of his game and went to Mount Kailash to meet his mother for lunch.

When he arrived home, the house was quiet. Lord Ganesha poked his head through the door. His mother was not in the kitchen. He passed to the back of the house and entered the garden. His mother was not there. He walked through the halls and found her huddled in a corner, covered in deep, purple bruises.

"Mother!" cried Lord Ganesha, running to her side. "What has happened?"

"You hurt me, child." Parvati sighed deeply. "When you tossed me in the air, I fell to the ground and bruised myself."

"But Mother," said Lord Ganesha, anxious to reassure her. "I did not throw you in the air. I have only just arrived home."

"I was the cat you tossed in the village below. It was my coat you dirtied, my tail you tweaked, and my sides that you bruised."

Parvati winced and paused to take her breath. Lord Ganesha bowed his head in shame.

"Mother, I am grieved. I know now that to injure another for entertainment is wrong and hurtful."

Great tears slipped from Lord Ganesha's eyes, and his tears moistened the floorboards near his mother's feet.

"It is a good lesson, child," said Parvati, rising. Lord Ganesha helped her to the kitchen and set before her a healing and hearty repast. Thus Lord Ganesha learned mercy and kindness to those smaller than he.

Chapter 10: Ganesha Wins a Race

Lord Ganesha and his brother, Karthikeya were very competitive. They jumped off stones to see who could leap the highest. They threw stones into the river to see who could splash the farthest. They even measured themselves against the trees to see who was the tallest.

One day, the gods gave the children a piece of special fruit from the gods. Its leaves were like fronds of silk, and its flesh was as delicious and milky as the cream from a cow. Both boys desired the fruit.

"It is mine!" cried Karthikeya. "I am the hungriest!"

"It is mine!" cried Ganesha. "I am the largest and need the most feeding!"

The boys fought until their parents separated them. Lord Shiva sought to restore peace.

"My children, you could share the fruit. Then both could taste its sweetness and be filled."

Lord Ganesha looked at Karthikeya. Karthikeya looked at Lord Ganesha.

"No!" they screamed together. "It is mine!"

Parvati sighed, but Lord Shiva smiled.

"Very well. Since you do not desire to share, each of you may have the opportunity to win the fruit. The first child to round the world three times wins the prize."

Karthikeya laughed and called his glorious peacock. Its feathers flashed once in the sunlight, and then Karthikeya and the peacock were gone, flying into the horizon.

Lord Ganesha sadly called his mount—the little mouse—and climbed on its back. The mouse ran as fast as it could, but it was tiny, and Lord Ganesha was very heavy. They had only gone a few feet before the mouse needed to stop for a rest. They travelled like that—the mouse and Lord Ganesha—for some time. After awhile, Lord Ganesha heard beating wings and turned as Karthikeya flew past.

"Ha, Brother!" Karthikeya cried, waving a stray peacock feather. "You might as well turn back. My mount is by far the fastest, and I will surely win the fruit!"

And Karthikeya's peacock disappeared again into the sky. Lord Ganesha sighed and turned his mouse toward home, sad already for the lost prize and Karthikeya's gloating.

As he neared home, he saw his parents—Lord Shiva and Parvati—waiting near the gate. A sudden idea occurred to him.

"Mother and Father," he said as he approached them. "May I round you three times since you are my world?"

Parvati smiled, and Lord Shiva nodded. Ganesha, on his little mouse, rounded his parents once. The little mouse stopped to rest. He rounded them twice. Karthikeya flapped by on his peacock and crowed his forthcoming victory. Lord Ganesha rounded his parents the third time.

Lord Shiva handed Lord Ganesha the fruit and blessed him for his insight. When Karthikeya arrived, he watched with a long face as the fruit disappeared into Lord Ganesha's stomach. Thus, Karthikeya earned his reward for gloating, and Lord Ganesha earned his for his wisdom.

Chapter 11: Shiva Skips Success

When Lord Ganesha was a small boy, Lord Shiva issued an important declaration on his son's behalf. Those who wished for success in any effort must first pay homage to Lord Ganesha. When a farmer strove in his fields and wished to bring in his harvest, he must reverence Lord Ganesha. When a servant sought a boon from his master, he must reverence Lord Ganesha.

"In no way may any receive success except by Lord Ganesha," he decreed. And it was so. Merchants offered prayers over their goods. Fathers prayed over their daughters and sons as they went forth to their marriages, and mothers prayed over their daughters as they brought forth children. All those who prayed to Lord Ganesha received success in their endeavors, and the name of Lord Ganesha was much loved.

Eventually, the demons in Tripura rose up in rebellion. They cursed the name of Shiva and threatened mortals and gods. Lord Shiva gathered his forces, bid farewell to his family, and started on his way. His forces marched for many days, and Lord Shiva bore his trident at their head. His mighty carriage rolled forth on the way to battle.

One day, Lord Shiva rode in his chariot, pondering over the upcoming battle. Crack! The carriage shook and jilted, throwing Lord Shiva awry. His soldiers ran to see what was the matter and lo! One of the pegs in the wheel had snapped.

"Ah!" said Lord Shiva. "It is just. For a while I decreed that all should pay homage to my son before success, I neglected my own words and did not offer my reverence as I ought."

Then Lord Shiva prayed to Lord Ganesha for success in his endeavor and gave repentance for his thoughtlessness. The soldiers of Lord Shiva fixed the peg and continued on their journey.

When they arrived in Tripura, the demons were many and restless. Their forms were dark and terrible, and their defiance set. Lord Shiva and his forces fought bravely and surely and turned the tide of the battle. The demons were subdued, and Lord Shiva returned home in safety.

Thus, Lord Shiva learned to honor his own word with the same homage that he paid to his son.

Chapter 12: Ravana's Ten Heads

There once was a scholar who was more learned than any other. He spent years mastering the Vedas and the Shastras and explored the mysteries of the universe. He plucked the veena until it played like the sound of a thousand birds singing. He wrote complex works about the stars that moved in the heavens and the medicine necessary to prolong life. He studied and learned until there was no theory left for him to master. But still, he was both mortal and vulnerable. He decided to seek a boon from the gods.

He meditated standing on one toe, and although wind and the rain smote him to and fro, he did not move. Still, the gods were silent. He fasted for a thousand years, long enough to forget the taste of food and the freshness of water. Still, his tapasya was unheard. Finally, he began to slice off his heads, and with each head lost part of himself.

He sliced off the first head, and with it sacrificed the ahamkara, the love of one's self. The great head, matted with dark hair, rolled to the ground and settled near his feet. Still, the gods were silent. Another head sprouted in its place, and Ravana raised his sword to strike again.

He sliced off the second head, and out came moha, attachment to family and friends. Still, the heavens were silent, and a new head sprouted to replace the one lost.

He sliced off the third head and released the love of his perfect self, which led to paschyataap, penance or repentance.

He sliced off the fourth head and loosed krodha, the rage that causes harm in others.

He sliced off the fifth head and forewent ghrina, the burning hatred.

He sliced off the sixth head and surrendered bhaya, the terror of possibility.

He sliced off the seventh head and offered up irshya, the sting of jealousy.

He sliced off the eighth head and abandoned lobha, the greed for possessions.

He sliced off the ninth head and relinquished kama, the heat of lust.

He sliced off the tenth head and forfeited jaddata, the pull of inaction or inertia.

At last, ten heads lay piled at Ravana's feet, and he sat back, exhausted. He had nothing else to offer. Lord Brahma appeared next to the pile of mangled offerings. He greeted Ravana respectfully.

"Ravana, I have heard your oblations and accept them. Do you seek a boon from me?"

"Haan ji, Lord Brahma," said Ravana, and he bowed himself to the ground. "I have sought power in the Vedas and the Shastras, and in great learning. But still, I am vulnerable. I wish to be made immortal and to become as one of the gods."

Lord Brahma heard and sighed, shaking his head.

"Though your penance and learning were both profound, Ravana, this gift is beyond my inclination to give. However, I will make you a promise that will cover in part your vulnerability: no god or demon will have the power to seek your life."

Ravana smiled. "This boon I will seek."

And when he had spoken his words, the ten heads of Ravana revived and grew more swart and tough than before. The sprouted anew from his broad shoulders, and arms spring out to serve them. Ravana took up arms and became the king of the rakshasas (the maneaters who plagued Lord Brahma at the beginning of the world).

Thus, Ravana became the greatest terror on the earth and in the heaven and ravaged the home of the gods.

Chapter 13: The Birth of Rama

Ravana, king of the rakshasas, terrorized the world. He made war on the mortal realms, slaying the people and seizing their riches and lands. He even distressed the gods and threatened to oust them from their prominence, for Lord Brahma had promised that god or demon could never slay him.

As Ravana's ravages spread, the gods appeared in council before Lord Brahma. Lord Indra, the god of highest heaven and wielder of storms, turned his face to the others.

"We have seen, o holy ones, the terror of Ravana, king of the rakshasas. He has destroyed our people and our shrines and threatens to destroy the footings of heaven itself."

The other gods murmured among themselves. Their worry broke like a wave over the feet of Lord Indra.

"This threat," he continued, "concerns all gods and demons who do not wish to pay homage to Ravana, nor forfeit the world to his hunger. But he is beyond our ability to injure. The sun shields his rays in fear of Ravana. The fire itself shrinks from the footsteps of Ravana. What, then, must be done?"

Lord Brahma sighed and was grieved by the suffering of men and gods, for Lord Brahma is the creator, and cares much for his creations.

"It is true that many are afflicted, and suffer greatly at the hands of Ravana. It is also true that he is protected by a boon he sought and now abuses."

The gods moaned and cast down their heads. Lord Brahma meditated within himself.

"Perhaps," he continued thoughtfully, "we may yet find a way to slay Ravana and cast his influence out. Though he did supplicate a boon of protection from me and though neither god nor demon may harm him, yet a man born of woman escapes those conditions."

Then hope infused the gods, for they saw not all was lost. Just then came Lord Vishnu, bearing his mace and discus and clothed in robes of saffron. His mount, the mighty eagle, alighted near Lord Brahma. The other gods did him reverence and welcomed him with gladness.

"Why, my friends, have I been prayed here? What task is there for me to do on behalf of the world?"

The gods explained their anxiety and the depravity of Ravana. Lord Vishnu's brow knit with concern.

"Lord Brahma, I have heard of the plague of Ravana and the horror of his ravishings. I will descend to the earth and become a man, that I may cast down Ravana and end the swath of his atrocity."

Then the gods rejoiced again as hope burned yet brighter. Truly Lord Vishnu, the great Madhava, and protector of worlds, could save them from the vexation of Ravana.

Then the Maruts, the winds, brought Indra tidings.

"A great king among men supplicated for a son," they said. "Dasaratha, this king, seeks knowledge and blessings from Brahma, the creator of all."

Lord Brahma nodded approvingly.

"Lord Vishnu shall descend to the family of Dasaratha and bless him with four sons. These sons shall defend both heaven and the world and bring an end to Ravana and his armies."

Lord Vishnu bowed his acceptance. The gods sent a messenger to Dasaratha, who was overjoyed to receive so honored a son. To prepare his wives to bear the sacred children, the gods sent a vase filled with holy nectar. Queen Kausalya consumed half, and Queen Sumitra and Queen Kaikeyi consumed a quarter each.

Thus Queen Kausalya conceived a bore Rama, the hero of the world.

Chapter 14: Urmila's Slumber

Rama, the son of Dasaratha and Kausalya, grew great in knowledge of war and wisdom. The time came for Dasaratha to choose between his sons and ordain which would follow him on the throne and lead the people in peace. Manthara, the waiting woman of Kaikeyi, spun dark and twisted tales of betrayal and destruction once Rama received the crown. Kaikeyi and her child, Bharata, would be ousted, she said. If she wished to escape destruction for her and her line, she must place Bharata first, even before Shatrughna and Lakshman. The young queen appeared before King Dasaratha.

"My Lord," she said, and her heart resounded with Manthara's twisted words. "Many years ago, you promised me a boon that I never received. I ask it now. Place Bharata on the throne, that he may be king after you and lead our people to peace."

Then King Dasaratha sorrowed because his heart ached for Rama and his leadership.

"Would you ask me this boon when you know it cost me my heart to bestow it?"

Queen Kaikeyi would not rescind her request, thanks to the whispers of Manthara, and so the king was bound to keep his word. Accordingly, Bharata was anointed king, and Rama sent into exile for fourteen years. Tormented by his promise, King Dasaratha died of a broken heart. Bharata refused to rule and placed Rama's silk slippers on the throne instead, in preparation for the day when the true king would return to bless the people.

All grieved when they heard the fruit of Manthara's wicked words. Rama bore the sad news to his lovely wife, Sita.

"My dear," said he. "We must forsake the riches and privilege of my father's palace, for I am bound to obey his commands. We will live in the jungle, in exile, until we may return once again to our home in Ayodhya."

Sita smiled, and her beauty glowed like the sun. She kissed her husband.

"I am not afraid," she said. "I will go with you."

Then Lakshman, the brother of Rama, mourned even more deeply. He would not be parted from Rama, even in exile.

"I wish to protect him if I can," Lakshman told his wife. "At least from some of the dangers of the jungle I may shield him if I accompany him into exile."

"Then go," said Urmila, the wife of Lakshman. "It is honorable to defend the son of Kausalya and even more honorable still to join him in trial as well as pleasure."

"But how will I protect him from harm?" asked Lakshman. "I am, but one man and the dangers of the jungle do not sleep."

"I will sleep on your behalf," said Urmila, "that you may dedicate both day and night to the protection of Rama and Sita."

Lakshman kissed his wife in gratitude and made preparations to leave. When the son of Kausalya left his home in Ayodhya, Lakshman went with them, bidding his faithful wife farewell.

Thus for fourteen years he guarded Rama and Sita, and passed with them through jungle, danger, battle, and death; and, for fourteen years Urmila slept on her couch in Ayodhya, that her husband might fulfill his duty.

Chapter 15: Deer of Deception

For many years Rama lived in the jungle with his beloved Sita and his brother, Lakshman, waiting to return to Ayodhya and regain his rightful crown. They fetched fruit from the trees and wove baskets from the fronds. The days Rama and Sita spent in happiness in each other's company, and the nights they spent under the watchful eye of Lakshman, who guarded them faithfully. Their friend, Jatayu, the eagle, kept watch for them also.

After a little more than thirteen years, Sita went to fetch water one day and noticed a mysterious deer. His antlers sparkled, and his coat shone with gold flecks. Sita tried to go after it, but the deer skittered away.

"Rama," said Sita, coming with the water jug and pointing to the trees. "A deer of gold runs in the fringe of the wood. He is beautiful, and his coat shines like polished gold."

Rama looked to the trees and spied the deer grazing near the roots. His heart shifted within him, and he frowned.

"I do not look kindly on this deer, my Sita. My heart is ill at ease that he should appear so near to our house and tempt you after him."

"But is he not beautiful?" Sita insisted. "I wish that you would get him for me."

Rama hesitated.

"I do not like him, either, Lord Rama," said Lakshman, eying the deer with his bow on his shoulder, ever ready to defend Rama and Sita. "My heart, too, sits ill when I look over his beauty, great as it is."

Sita sighed and looked after the deer longingly. She had not asked for riches, nor for privilege in her exile, though she was a queen among women. Rama looked upon his wife and ached for her disappointment. He forgot the warning in his heart and sought only to please Sita.

"I will fetch the deer," he said, stringing his bow, "to please Sita and to bring her a gift. If there be any evil about this deer, it is my duty to address it."

Lakshman made to accompany Rama, to protect him in the forest. Rama held up his hand.

"Stay, my brother, while I seek this deer. Would I leave Sita here alone and unprotected?"

"It is my wish to accompany you," said Lakshman, still watching the mysterious deer. "I fear the forest and the temptings of this golden creature."

"I am grateful, my brother," said Rama. "But my life is empty if my Sita is not safe. I will not venture far, and will return shortly."

Then, Lakshman, ill at ease, took up guard outside the cottage of Rama and Sita, and Rama pursued the deer into the woods. The deer darted between trees and around twisted roots, obscuring Rama's shots and drawing him deeper into the forest. Finally, Rama launched a shaft that lodged in the deer, and it stumbled to the ground.

But when Rama approached, the deer revealed himself as Maricha, the demon, who laughed at Rama for his deception.

"Ha! Prince of Ayodhya with no more sense than a beetle! My work is done well, and your precious Sita is lost."

Before Rama could reply, Maricha cried out in voice of Rama.

"Help! Help! I perish! O, Sita! O Lakshman!"

At the cottage, the cries of Maricha sunk into Sita's heart.

"Oh, my husband!" she cried. "Go, Lakshman, and aid him, lest he die alone in the darkness of the jungle!"

"There are none who may harm Rama when he is armed with manavastra, his magic bow," said Lakshman, though his face was worried. Sita was not appeased.

"Oh, go quickly, Lakshman, lest I lose my husband and king both!"

Reluctantly, Lakshman obeyed and set off for the jungle. Then Sita was left alone, and her worries preyed upon her.

"Oh my husband, my Rama! Would that he is safe!"

She prayed many prayers in the cottage, waiting for Lakshman and Rama to return. The sound of footsteps tapped against her ears, and she ran to the door. It was only a poor beggar, seeking alms from the beautiful princess. Sita sighed in disappointment but ran inside to seek alms for the beggar.

As she placed the alms in his hand, he grasped her arm like the grip of death. She cried out and struggled but Ravana, who was the beggar in disguise, only laughed and pulled her to his flying chariot.

"Now you shall be my wife and not the wife of a poor beggar who can neither preserve nor protect you."

"O, Rama! O Lakshman!" Sita screamed as she was born into the air. Jatayu, the eagle, tried to interfere but was cut down by Ravana. Sita, weeping, was born away to Lanka, the island of Ravana, and many nights spent Rama seeking her and pining her loss.

Thus perished Maricha, the trickster demon who deceived Rama and aided Ravana.

Chapter 16: Hanuman's Torch

All were horrified by Sita's captivity. The birds cried out in the canopies and told tales of her beauty and abduction. The monkeys and bears aided Rama in his search, seeking Sita on mountains, in rivers, and over hills. Even Hanuman, the son of Vayu, helped Rama. It was he who finally found Sita imprisoned in the fortress of Ravana.

Hanuman, son of the wind, stood with the army of Rama and looked across the sea to the island of Lanka. There sat the fortress of Ravana, and there, too, sat Sita, imprisoned somewhere inside. How Rama ached for his wife! They had searched for many days and nights without food or rest, and now an impassable ocean divided him and his Sita.

Hanuman was moved with pity for Rama.

"Oh, that I could seek Sita across the waves! How gladly would I fly to her aid for Rama's sake!"

Jambavantha, the bear king, spoke.

"Hanuman, you have forgotten your heritage and abilities. As a child, you plagued the sages and distracted them from their meditations. To preserve their peace, they cursed you with forgetfulness. You are the son of Vayu, the wind, and may fly as he does if you wish."

Then the curse was lifted from Hanuman, and the memory of his abilities surged in him. He heaped from the shore with a scream and soared over the waves to the fortress of Ravana.

He landed near the gates and forced his way past the door guard, but nowhere could he find Sita, whom he knew only by description. He passed the beauties of Ravana's court. Sita was not there. He passed the banquet halls and dark dungeons. Sita was not there, either. Despairing, Hanuman hopped from tree to tree in the gardens. The sound of weeping touched his ears. Under the trees and heavy blossoms, he found Sita, worn thin with worry and the pang of her captivity. She wept for Rama even as fierce demons chastised and abused her.

The sight tore at Hanuman's heart. He waited until an opportune moment and then approached Sita.

"Beautiful princess of Mithila, have hope! Deliverance is soon at hand."

But Sita turned away from him. Too well she knew the torments and false encouragement from the servants of Ravana and suspected Hanuman as another of these. But Hanuman was determined to do her service, if he may. He dropped a shining ring into Sita's hand.

"Look, fair Sita, upon the ring given to you by your faithful husband, Rama. I have brought it as proof both of his devotion and my authenticity as his messenger."

Then Sita smiled and wiped away her tears. She thanked Hanuman for his comfort in her distress. The demons that guarded her returned at this moment and strove with Hanuman. Sita cried out and prayed for his protection. Hanuman fought valiantly, though outnumbered, and caused the demons much anxiety; at length, he was captured and dragged before Ravana.

Hanuman could almost admire the ten-headed sage, so great and marvelous was his court. Then he thought of Rama's grief, and of Sita's tear-stained face.

"What do you here, spy?" asked Ravana gruffly. "Do you come as an emissary from Indra?"

"No," said Hanuman boldly. "I come on behalf of Rama, the prince of Ayodhya, whose wife you have stolen in the basest of crimes. In his name, I demand her return."

"Rama? Ha!" laughed Ravana. "I have stolen what I deserve and recognize no claim from a prince of men."

"Then face your own destruction," said Hanuman. "For though you are immune to both gods and demons, by a man you might yet be killed, and Rama will surely do so unless you return his wife."

Then Ravana called for the death of Hanuman. Ravana's advisors counseled him vigorously, warning him against further unconscionable action.

"Very well," said Ravana. "I will punish him fit for his station. The tail is dearest to a monkey. Burn it!"

The cruel demons shrieked with joy and hurried to carry out the dark order. They wrapped Hanuman's tail with fuel and dragged him through the streets, mocking him and his mission. Then the prayer of Sita intervened on his behalf. Though his tale burned, the heat did not mar him. The flames flickered brightly but did not consume him. Then Hanuman caused his tail to grow until it crackled as merrily as a torch.

"I will leave the mark of Rama," he thought, "and inflict their punishment upon themselves."

Then Hanuman leaped to the rooftops, escaping his captors. He sprung from eave to eave, passing his tail over house and tree. The flames grasped the city until all but Sita's bower was smothered in smoke. Then Hanuman dipped his tail in the ocean, and the waves extinguished the flames.

Thus Hanuman torched Lanka and carried Rama's ultimatum to Ravana, Sita's captor.

Chapter 17: Suvannamachha Steals a Bridge

When Hanuman returned, he told Rama of his exploits and why the smoke floated on the horizon. He assured the prince that Sita was safe and that Ravana would not release her for any prize or persuasion. Rama sorrowed. But the armies of King Jambavantha and the brethren of Hanuman cried out for justice, and both the smoke of ravaged Lanka and the cries of his friends cheered Rama's heart.

"We must rescue my beloved and release her from her torment," said Rama. "But how can we pass over this great water? We have no ships to sail, and the distance is too far to swim."

"Lord Rama, petition Varuna," offered Lakshman. "Surely the lord of the ocean will hear us and help to make a way."

And so Rama prayed, but Varuna would not hear his prayers for fear of Ravana. After some persuasion, Varuna offered the services of an architect serving in his army. Nala could build a bridge to carry Rama's army across the waves. Under Nala's direction, the troops uprooted trees and boulders and tossed them into the sea. Throngs of bears hurled boulders into the sea to form the footings of the bridge. One by one, the rocks crashed into the waves, raising the foundations that much higher.

After a day of effort, the armies noticed a disturbing trend. No matter how many rocks sunk beneath the waves, the bridge progressed no further. The bears sought larger boulders, and the monkeys uprooted greater trees. But the bridge did not advance.

"There is trickery here," said Lakshman, watching the waves. "Something flickers in the depths."

Hanuman stepped forward.

"Send me beneath the waves, Lord Rama," he said. "I will seek the trickster and remove the barriers."

Lord Rama agreed, and Hanuman marched into the waves. He pushed through the water, down deeper and deeper to the ocean floor. Finally, he saw movement in the depths and hid behind a rock to watch.

A troop of enchanting mermaids flitted near the footings of the bridge. When a new boulder descended to the depths, they hauled it away. A mermaid even lovelier than her cohorts watched the process, directing their efforts.

"So!" thought Hanuman angrily. "The bridge does not progress because of these minions, no doubt sent by Ravana to prevent Rama's crossing."

The Hanuman burst from behind his boulder and swam toward the most beautiful, scattering the others in his path.

As he pursued her, Hanuman noticed the mermaid's beauties—the caress of her hair in the current, the flash of her eyes like the sun on the sea.

"Who are you?" he asked, stung by the pangs of love and forgetting the bridge for a moment.

"Suvannamachha," she replied, and her voice was like the echo of bells. "I am the daughter of Ravana."

Then Hanuman remembered his mission and the army hampered by her interference.

"Though my heart aches for you, fair mermaid, yet I am bound to a more serious task. Ravana has captured the wife of Rama and holds her captive on Lanka. It is to rescue her that we construct this bridge."

Then Suvannamaccha was grieved by her father's doings and blessed the construction of the bridge. Her mermaids returned the rocks they had removed, and the bridge progressed again. Hanuman stayed with her for a short time before he returned to the surface. When Savannamaccha bid him goodbye, her eyes returned his love.

"Farewell, son of Vayu, and most handsome of the monkey race. Me and my helpers will guard the bridge from below, so no other may hinder its progress."

Then Hanuman returned to the shore, and Lord Rama congratulated him on his success. Ever after the heart of Hanuman remembered the voice of a beauty beneath the sea.

After five days, the bridge reached Lanka, and the army passed to dry ground at last.

So was built Rama Setu, Rama's Bridge, with the help of Suvannamachha, the daughter of Ravana.

Chapter 18: Hanuman Moves a Mountain

When the bears and monkeys reached Lanka, they pounded the walls of the city with their fists.

"Ha!" said mighty Ravana, and his mouth gaped open like a chasm. "I do not fear these monkeys. I will keep Sita as my own, though it costs me the city of Lanka and everything in it."

His generals and advisors saw the bears and monkeys assaulting the walls, and their nerves trembled with the shaking stones.

"Return Sita, Great Lord!" they cried. "The vultures already circle your capital. The omens predict your downfall. Undo your evil deed and save our beautiful city!"

"Silence!" cried Ravana. "I will not return Sita, after all, I have sacrificed to get and keep her. I will destroy Rama and his armies as easily as the wind strips the leaves from trees!"

Then Ravana's counselors trembled and were silent. Vibhishana, the brother of Ravana, found him deaf to good counsel, and followed dharma to the camp of Rama, seeking refuge. But Ravana cared not. Driven nearly mad by his desire for Sita and restrained by Brahma's curse, he simmered in her rejection and thought of nothing else.

When the forces outside the gate cried for battle, Ravana prepared to deliver it. He sent his greatest generals. Indrajit rode to battle in his war chariot, followed by his brother, Prahasta. Trishira rode forth without fear, all three of his heads cursing Rama and Lakshman for their audacity.

When the two forces clashed, the sound was like mountains crumbling into one another. Rakshasha, monkey, and bear clawed and tore at the enemy, littering the battlefield with the dead and wounded. In the name of Ravana Dhumraksha, Akampana, and Kumbhakarna strode into the melee, and their steps shook the ground. But Hanuman, Angada, Nila, and Nala returned the arrows of the accursed, and massacred Ravana's generals one by one. So dire was the battle that Rama and Lakshman were struck down. Finally, the forces retreated, and the armies were left to sort among the fallen.

Among the wounded, the forces of Rama found Jambavantha, the bear king.

"Hanuman!" he cried. "Where is Hanuman?"

"How do you cry for Hanuman before seeking first after Rama's safety?" asked Vibhishana.

"Only Hanuman can save Rama and Lakshman, for if I have fallen, so surely have they, too."

Then Hanuman was called and came to the bear king.

"What would you, good king?" he asked. "Rama and Lakshman are wounded, and I would help them if I could."

"Listen," said the king. "In the Himalayas, there is a mountain called Mahodaya, the home of sweet herbs and healing. On the slopes, you will find the herbs growing, caressed by the breath of heaven. Return with them quickly that Lakshman and Rama might be healed."

With a great cry, Hanuman sprang into the sky. Quick as the wind he brushed the treetops of the sprawling forests and skipped across the sands of the vast deserts. He bowed in reverence as he passed Mount Kailash, the home of Shiva, but too quickly did he fly to offer any obeisance more. Finally, his toes touched the hallowed mountain. But oh! Thousands of plants covered the mountainside. Which were the ones that might heal Rama and Lakshman? Hanuman dashed from flower to flower, sniffing each by turn.

"The Prince of Ayodhya suffers, and I cannot help him!" cried Hanuman. "Mount Mahodaya, aid me in my search!"

But the mountain was silent. The words of Hanuman echoed off the boulders and bounced back to his face.

"So be it!" he shouted. "If you will not help me, I will take you along!"

Then Hanuman seized the mountaintop and held it like a platter, passing back over desert and forest until he reached the island of Lanka. No sooner had the mountaintop passed over the sea than the breezes wafted over the injured princes and healed their wounds. Jambavantha, too, and the other warriors of Rama's forces received strength and praised the great deed of Hanuman.

Thus, were Rama and Lakshman saved, and the mountaintop of Mayodaya was removed.

Chapter 19: The Final Battle

One by one, the great generals of Lanka were defeated. The kinsmen of Ravana perished under the arrows of Rama. His sons fell to the lance of Lakshman. When Indrajit and his magnificent chariot were conquered, Ravana's rage knew no bounds. He tore the tapestries from his walls and threw down the gold and jewels from their sconces. In his fury, he donned his armor and sword and sought Sita's life, she for whom he had suffered so much.

On his way to her bower, he met one of his advisors, who counseled him.

"Lord Ravana," he said, "There is still yet time and opportunity for you to avenge your sons and kinsmen. The princes of Ayodhya still live, waiting to receive your wrath."

Then the rage of Ravana turned from Sita and toward Rama and his army. "They desecrate the shores of Lanka with their feet and provoke my anger with their defiance!" he cried. "I will descend and finish them personally."

Then the great chariot of Ravana rolled forth as a tongue of fire, and the bears and monkeys quailed before it. Rama saw him come and called to him across the field of shattered spears and broken foes.

"Ravana!" he said, brandishing his bow. "You are come to be punished for your heinous deed, the capture of my wife. But not only this act hangs over you. The fruits of your wrath—the assaults against the sages and Devas—have gone unanswered. Today you are accountable, and the reckoning will be swift."

Ravana hurled his scorn into the face of Rama with a laugh.

"I fear no god nor Deva, as none may harm me. As for Sita, I took only what I deserved, since I found her alone and unguarded by those who should have been her protectors. She is my conquest, and I claim her as my own."

The heart of Rama sickened with grief and indignation, but he answered calmly.

"I am no god nor Deva, but a man—a man whose wife you have stolen. Since you will not return her, I will lay you to waste and seek her myself."

Then Ravana's blood ran cold, and he realized how craftily he had been lured and how blindly his pride had guided him. But even now he would not be swayed, for the thought of Sita and the agony of defeat goaded him.

"Then come," he cried, "and meet your death."

Ravana jumped on his chariot and ordered his charioteer to run Rama down. Hanuman sprang to Rama's side.

"If it please you, Great Lord," he said, humbly. "Ride on my back that you and the demon king might fight on equal footing."

Then Rama blessed him and rode to battle on the back of Hanuman. The conflict rocked the island of Lanka. The astras, the weapons of the gods, rang as Rama and Ravana rained blow after blow upon the head of their opponent. The bow of Rama sang as he sped arrow after arrow in the heads of Ravana, and the sword of Ravana clanged as it sought the heart of Rama. But no matter how many arrows Rama fired, the heads of Ravana regrew and multiplied, and he fought on.

"Great Prince," said Hanuman, wearing with running across the battlefield. "Remember that Ravana hides the nectar of immortality in his navel and that only the shot of a man may spill it out."

Then Rama drew his mightiest arrow and fit it to his bow. With his breath, he drew in the universe and with his string he released it. The mighty arrow struck true, and the nectar of immortality spilled from the navel of Ravana. He fell with a cry, and his fall shook the whole earth.

Thus, Rama defeated Ravana, the demon king of the Rakshasas.

Chapter 20: Sita's Purity

After the downfall of Ravana, the army of Rama celebrated. The monkeys leaped in the air, and the bears chanted, "Victory to Sri Rama! Victory to Sita, the wife of Sri Rama, released from captivity!"

Then Rama remembered the captivity of Sita and the lust of Ravana, and his heart grew cold. The words of Ravana echoed in his mind, and his heart grew colder still.

"Bring Sita to me," he said to Hanuman, and the monkey was surprised by his tone. "Let her come to me on foot."

Then Vibhishana led Sita from the city. She was worn and thin from sorrow, but her eyes shone with devotion. She rushed to Rama, Sita the lotus-eyed princess. But Rama looked away.

"For many months you have rested in a stranger's home, and so you are a stranger to me. I release you from your marriage vow, and free you to seek another husband."

The monkeys gasped, and the bears groaned and covered their eyes. Even Sugriva, the king thirsty for justice, kept his peace and was grieved. The eyes of Sita filled with tears.

"Oh my husband, my Rama! How could you accuse me of such things? Ravana forced his touch upon me in my abduction, and I abhorred and shunned it during the length of my captivity. Can you doubt my devotion to you?"

But Rama still looked away, and his lips drew into a line as stiff as the horizon. Then Sita's heart broke, and the tears spilled from her eyes and down her flawless cheeks.

"Lakshman," she said, forcing the grief from her throat. "Build me a pyre upon which to burn myself. If Rama will not take me as his wife, then my life is worth nothing but to be taken."

Then Lakshman looked beseechingly to Rama, his brother, pleading for Sita with his eyes. But still, Rama was silent and nodded his consent. Lakshman built the pyre and set it ablaze. The flames licked hungrily at the logs. Sita turned to the assembled bears, monkeys, and generals.

"Hear my testimony!" she cried and drew herself up. "If I am impure and unfaithful to my husband, the flames will consume me, and neither he nor I will suffer more."

"O Sita!" cried the bears, and their tears washed the bloody field.

"O Sita!" cried the monkeys, and their cries echoed from the skies.

Then Lakshman fell to his knees and wept, and Hanuman hid his face. But Rama was silent still, though his heart ached within him.

Sita jumped into the pyre, and the flames took her. Then the heart of Rama broke, and the tears spilled from his eyes. The sobs wracked his chest, and he fell to the ground in despair.

At this moments the gods descended, and Brahma himself pulled Sita from the fire. He hair shone with luster, and her eyes sparkled with love and purity. Brahma presented her to Rama.

"Behold your wife, Lord Rama. She is pure beyond the fire's ability to consume her. Accept her to yourself without fear or apprehension. The separation is at an end."

Then Rama ran to Sita and took her in his arms, and called her his wife.

Thus was Sita tested and proved worthy beyond the power of fire.

Chapter 21: Krishna Steals Butter

Many years ago, Devaki gave birth to a baby boy and called him Krishna. To hide him from his uncle, Devaki delivered him to Yashoda, who cared for him as her son. Krishna loved Yashoda as his mother but didn't always obey her.

Once, when he had grown into a small child, Krishna stole a pat of butter. What sweetness! What goodness! His infant tongue yearned for more. He started slipping small pieces of butter onto his plate during meals and snuck into the kitchen during the day to taste his new favorite food. Shortly after that, there was no butter left in the house since Krishna had eaten it all.

Yashoda laughed and sighed in the same breathe, for it was impossible to be angry with such an audacious and loving child.

"Krishna," she said, waving her finger. "It is not well to eat all of the butter, for then there is none for us to cook with. Please stay away from the butter."

But Krishna's taste for butter could not be stemmed by Yashoda's words. Soon he stole butter from all of the neighbors, as well, and eventually from everyone in Vrindavan. They knocked on Yashoda's door, and she listened to their complaints.

"Krishna ate my butter, and now I have none for my bread!" cried the baker, with his face covered in flour.

"Krishna ate my butter, and now I have none to cook my fish!" cried the angler, his elbows dripping with seawater.

"Krishna ate my butter, and now I have none for my children!" cried the mothers with downcast faces and wagging fingers.

Yashoda sighed, for she was tired of Krishna's naughty butter habit. She proposed a clever solution.

"To keep the butter from Krishna, tie it high up in a pitcher beyond where he can reach. Then the butter will be safe, and Krishna will not be able to steal it."

The people of Vrindavan heeded Yashoda and hung the pitchers high in their kitchens. Soon Krishna had no source of butter to quench his sweet tooth and was very put out.

One day, Yashoda left home to run an errand.

"Play safely until I return," she said, "and I shall give you a treat."

As soon as she was gone, naughty Krishna gathered all of his little friends. He pointed to the pitcher high above their heads.

"There, high above us, is a pitcher of butter. If we work together, then we can get the butter and enjoy the treat together. There is no need to wait until Yashoda returns."

The friends of Krishna clapped their hands and agreed to help him. They formed a bridge with their little arms and legs, and Krishna used them as a ladder to climb up to the butter. Ah, the golden goodness! Ah, the sweetest treat! The children enjoyed it very much, licking each spoonful clean and then dipping again for another. Laughing over their victory, they didn't hear Yashoda return. She saw the children with the butter pitcher and dirty spoons and clapped her hands to her head.

"Krishna!" she cried. "You have disobeyed me and led your friends to mischief. You shall be punished."

Then the friends of Krishna deserted him and ran from the kitchen, dropping their dirty spoons and guilty consciences by the way. Then Yashoda took Krishna and spanked him, to punish him for stealing the butter and for leading his friends astray.

Thus Lord Krishna learned the hard way to obey his elders and to honor his friends.

Chapter 22: Krishna Trades for Jewels

On another occasion, Krishna sat playing on the doorstep while his mother completed the chores. A woman passed by their home, selling delicious, plump fruit.

"Camachile, Carambola, Buddha's Hand—delicious fruits for sale," she cried.

Little Krishna looked longingly at her basket. He saw mellow langsat and imagined their bittersweet flavor. He saw purple mangosteen and sweet persimmons and yearned for the piquant ambarella.

"Ah," he thought, "If only I could taste the pink karonda or the glossy bilimbi. My mouth waters for a taste."

Krishna grabbed a handful of grains with which to trade and sprinted joyfully into the street. But the grains slipped from his little fingers as he ran, and when he arrived at the fruit basket, all of his grains were gone. Then little Krishna's eyes filled with tears and his lip trembled, for he had nothing wherewith to trade for the fruit. The fruit woman saw his sorrow and took his little hand in hers.

"Precious child!" she said. "You may take as many fruits as you like. Here, see the ripe targola. They will fit perfectly in your grip."

"But I have nothing with which to buy the fruits," said Krishna sadly, showing his empty palms. But the woman smiled.

"Whatever you have in your hands is enough for me. I accept your offering and bid you take what you like."

Then the kind fruit woman gave Krishna whatever fruits his heart desired, and he rejoiced over the dark phalsa berries and the golden mimusops. He thanked her and hugged her around the neck before skipping back to his front porch. She smiled and continued on her way.

She hadn't gone far, however, before she reached into her basket for some more fruit and bumped her fingers on hard stones. In amazement, she reached into her basket and drew forth rubies, emeralds, diamonds, and pearls. The woman gasped and dug further into the basket, which filled further with sapphires set in silver and jade set in gold.

The woman dropped to her knees and offered reverence to Vishnu for sending her a mighty gift. All the while Krishna smiled, enjoying his fruit on the doorstep.

Thus was the fruit woman rewarded for her kindness to Krishna and her devotion to Vishnu.

Chapter 23: Krishna Swallows the Flames

When Krishna grew older, his mother trusted him to tend their cows in the jungle. He and his friends drove their herds deep into the trees and undergrowth, and then played games while the cows ate their fill.

Krishna and his friends played Vish Amrit and Langdi, but Lagori, the game of stacked stones, was their favorite. Krishna stacked the rocks in a pile and then gave the ball to his friends. They threw it, knocking over the stones. Krishna rushed to the pile, stacking them up again while they tried to hit him with the ball. He was too quick, and soon all of them were laughing together.

Meanwhile, at the edge of the forest, a farmer fell asleep over his cook fire. The fire crept away and spread to the trees, consuming all in its path. Krishna's friends did not see the fire creeping behind them.

"Hit him again," they cried. "Knock out the rocks!"

Finally, the smoke drifted over them, and the cows stampeded in fear. Krishna's friends fell on their faces and wailed.

"Fire is come!" they cried. "Save us, Krishna! Save us!"

Then Krishna looked up from the game for the first time and saw the flames licking, his friends wailing, and the cows stampeding. He answered his friends calmly.

"Close your eyes," he commanded. "And I will save you."

"What?" said his friends. "What do you mean?"

"Close your eyes and do not open them again until I give you leave," said Krishna.

Then the friends of Krishna closed their eyes and put their hands over their faces, whimpering. Krishna drew in a breath as deep as the sea and swallowed all the fire. He swallowed the fire dancing in the trees. He swallowed the fire sneaking through the grasses. He swallowed the fire terrorizing the cows. When every snippet of the fire was gone, Krishna bid his friends open their eyes.

"Arise," he said. "Open your eyes."

His friends arose and peered around the clearing. The fire was gone, and the cows were saved. Even the smell of smoke was stolen from the breeze.

"Glory to Vishnu!" they cried. "Honor to Krishna and his mighty breath!"

Then Krishna and his friends gathered their cows and returned safely to their homes.

Thus Krishna preserved his friends and swallowed the fire that endangered them.

Chapter 24: Agni Spreads a Curse

Sage Bhrigu cursed Agni on behalf of his wife. In terror, Agni fled and concealed himself from God and man. Soon, the gods sent out a search party to find him. Agni jumped into the ocean and hid beneath the waves.

"They will never find me here," he thought. "The waves are too deep, and even my flames are quenched here."

But his fire burned hotter than he imagined, and soon the fish fled and the whales toned their displeasure. The frogs went to the gods and requested their aid.

"Remove Agni from the ocean, for he boils us with his heat."

The gods came to remove Agni, but he fled, cursing the frogs as he went.

"Because you have revealed me, you shall lose your sense of taste," he said. "Let that teach your tongues to wag."

Then Agni escaped the gods and took refuge in a banyan tree. The deep canopy shielded him from the sky, and the twisted roots and trailing branches hid him from view.

"Ah," thought Agni. "They won't possibly find me here. The branches are too close, and the roots reach too deep."

But a passing elephant reached into the banyan tree for his food and burned his trunk.

"Ouch!" he cried. "This banyan tree is burning!"

Then the elephant went to the gods and told them the story of the banyan tree and his burnt trunk.

"Remove Agni from the banyan tree," said the elephant, "for he burns me and I will starve."

The gods came to remove Agni, but he fled, cursing the elephant as he went.

"Because you have revealed me, you shall have a short tongue. Let that teach you to tell tales that aren't your own."

Then Agni perched in a shami tree, thinking that perhaps his flames could resemble the blushing flower pods and keep him hidden. But a colorful pitta saw him there and thought he was stealing her favorite resting place.

"Agni perches in the shami tree," she chirped. "Agni steals my favorite perch."

Then the pitta flitted to the gods and told them where Agni was hiding.

"Remove Agni from the shami tree," she asked, "for I am weary and need a place to rest."

The gods came to remove Agni, but he fled, cursing the pitta as he went.

"Because you have revealed me, you shall have a tongue that is cursed on the inside," he said. "Let that teach you to wag it too much."

Then the frogs, the elephant, and the pitta were grieved at the curses and made a ruckus in the land. The gods listened to their concerns and blessed them, each according to their worries.

The frogs, though they could no longer taste their way as did the snake, would be able to move gracefully even in darkness.

The elephant, though his tongue was short, could eat anything he wanted and lose his fear of starving to death.

The pitta, though her tongue was curved inside, could sing and warble to her heart's content. This gift of song spread to the other birds, who never forgot the curses of Agni and the gifts of the gods.

Thus Agni was found out by the animals and spread this discomfort among them.

Chapter 25: Vayu Humbles the Silk Cotton Tree

The mountains of the Himalayas stretch to the sky, a reminder of man's ascension to the Trimurti. On the slopes of these mountains grew the silk cotton tree, and its blossoms blessed the horizon. Year after year it grew larger, spreading its branches even further into the sky. Then the tree was happy in fulfilling its purpose and provided blossoms for all who passed by.

One day Narada, the storyteller, passed by with his khartal jingling. He sat beneath the silk cotton tree to rest and to play his instruments. The drone of his tambura pleased the tree, and it stood very still to hear each note and swell.

"How beautifully you play," said the tree. "Truly you are the master of Mahathi."

Narada smiled and bowed.

"Thank you. I have worked many years to master its ways."

Then the tree fell silent, wondering if it, too, could master something and earn glory in the world, as did Narada. It could not travel to the lokas, the hidden realms, but surely it could master its own gentle slope. In the meantime Narada rested his head at its roots and admired the tree, looking up into its steady branches.

"How great you have grown, silk cotton tree," he said. "Your branches that stretch toward the heavens are firm and strong. Not even a mighty storm could shake them."

"Ah," said the tree, thinking quickly. "I grow strong and firm because the storm is my servant. It knows better than to blow on its master."

Narada raised his eyebrows but said nothing. He thanked the tree for its shade and continued on his way. Later, he met Vayu, the god of wind and storms.

"Hello, Vayu!" he said. "I know you love a good story. You'll never believe what I heard the silk cotton tree say."

"Tell me, Narada," laughed Vayu, "for your stories are more entertaining than leaves dancing in a breeze."

Then Narada told Vayu what the silk cotton tree had said—that it was the master of the storm and therefore kept its leaves always because the wind could not shake its branches. Then the face of Vayu turned dour.

"What, does the silk cotton tree think itself so powerful?" he asked. "I'll show it in a moment where the truth lies."

Then Vayu flew to the Himalayas and confronted the tree, tousling its leaves with his breath.

"Hear, silk cotton tree. You are not the master of the storm. You spoke to bluster, but the breezes do not heed your command."

The proud tree refused to acknowledge its mistake and ignored Vayu. This only angered Vayu further. He blustered through the tree's branches.

"Listen, silk cotton tree. I do not blow on you out of respect for Brahma. When he created the world, he stopped to rest on one of your branches. It is his holiness and not your mastery that I honor."

Still, the tree kept its peace. Vayu's face darkened, and he worked himself into a great storm. The winds tore at the hillside and stripped the silk cotton tree of its blushing leaves and blossoms. The tree sighed over the leaves littering its roots, but could not return them to their places.

Thus the tree was punished for its arrogance and lost its leaves like every other.

Chapter 26: Savitri Chooses a Husband

Once, in the Madra Kingdom, there lived a king who longed for a child. He and his consort, Malavi, prayed and prayed for an heir to continue their line. At last, they were sent a daughter, and they named her Savitri.

Savitri grew up beautiful and pure. Her hair flowed like the river Ganges, and her lotus eyes smiled on all she saw. In fact, when the time came for her to marry, none sought her hand; she was too beautiful, too pure for any suitor in her land. Her father called her to him.

"My daughter," said King Ashwapati, "since none here seek your hand, you must seek your own husband. Find the son of a king for my sake, and for your own seek a man of noble heart."

"Thank you, my father," Savitri replied. "I will travel and search out a husband the best I may."

Then Savitri left her father's palace. She left behind her gold, her jewels, and her fine silk saris and took up a hermit's pack, replete with the necessary materials for her journey. She walked many miles, seeking a husband to meet her father's qualifications. After many days of travel, she came across a blind man in a forest, scratching near the roots of trees for food.

"Here, good hermit," she said, offering him some fruit. "Take some food from my pack that I may not be grieved by your hunger."

The hermit nodded gratefully and accepted the meal.

"And from what fair voice and hand do I receive so ample a gift?" he asked, as he devoured the meal.

"I am Savitri," she replied, "daughter of Ashwapati and Malavi."

"The princess?" said the blind man. "Ah, that I am blind! I had heard you described as a great beauty of open heart and mind. Could you describe yourself for me?"

Savitri tried, but couldn't give the hermit a clear description of herself. He smiled and called his son, Satyavan.

"My son," said the hermit. "Can you describe for me the Princess Savitri?"

Then Satyavan looked on the princess, and his heart yearned for hers in an instant. But he restrained himself and said instead, "Oh my father, she is as beautiful as the sun rising. Her eyes shine like the stars in the night sky, and her face is open to the tune of Dharma. Her hair flows like the sacred river, and the curve of her lips speaks peace and truth."

Then the heart of Savitri quivered in her, and she looked favorably on Satyavan.

"Oh," she thought, "that I could gratify my father as well as myself. Satyavan's heart knows the way of Dharma and his soul is open to truth."

Then Savitri sighed, and made to bid the hermit goodbye.

"Thank you for your conversation," she said, glancing at Satyavan, "but I must continue on my mission."

"Your mission?" asked the hermit. "What is that? And may we help?"

Then the heart of Savitri ached for Satyavan even more, and she sighed again.

"I seek a husband noble both in birth and in heart, for none have courage to woo me in my own country."

"Princess," said the hermit, bowing deeply. "Look favorably on my son, Satyavan. He is noble in both birth and in heart, for I am the King Dyumatsena of the Kingdom of Salwa. My eyesight and kingdom were taken from me, and I am left a hermit here in the forest. Bless my son, Satyavan, and consent to be his wife."

Then Princess Savitri smiled, and the brightness of her joy rivaled the light of the sun. King Dyumatsena placed her hand in the hand of Satyavan, and her heart knit with his.

Thus was Princess Savitri promised to Satyavan, son of King Dyumatsena.

Chapter 27: Savitri's Fidelity

When Savitri returned to her father's court, she found the shades of mourning hanging near the door and Narada, the storyteller and messenger of Vishnu, in audience.

She bowed deeply to her father and Narada and joyfully told them about her choice to marry Satyavan. Then Narada's face grew grave, and he rested his tambura upon the ground.

"Princess," he said. "You have made a poor decision. Satyavan is indeed noble both in birth and in heart, but his destiny is already writ before him. A year from today he will die, and you will be left husbandless as you were before."

"My daughter!" said King Ashwapati. "Please, choose another and spare yourself this aggravation."

But Princess Saravati drew herself up.

"I will choose a husband but once, and I have chosen Satyavan."

"So be it," said Narada, and he nodded approvingly. King Ashwapati was grieved, but granted the wish of Savitri. She and Satyavan made saptapadi, their vows in the presence of sacred fire, and their marriage began in peace. Savitri left behind the wealth of her childhood and donned the guise of a hermit, and lived happily with Satyavan in the forest.

A year passed. Each day seemed like a blink to Savitri, so deep was her love for her husband. Then finally arrived the day when Satyavan was predicted to die. Savitri asked permission to accompany him into the forest, and they entered with heavy hearts.

"Though I am to die," said Satyavan, picking up his axe, "I would leave you with enough wood to keep our home warm."

Savitri kissed his hand and bid him work. After a time, the face of Satyavan grew pale and strained, and he placed his head in Savitri's lap. She watered him with her tears as her heart choked within her breast.

Out of the trees came Yama himself, the god of the dead, sent to fetch the soul of Satyavan. Yama stripped the soul of Satyavan away and turned back into the forest, and the trees bent back to offer him passage. Savitri followed sadly, tracing the steps of Yama and following the soul of Satyavan. After a time, Yama noticed Savitri behind him.

"Princess," he said. "Turn back and take another husband, for the destiny of Satyavan is to die today."

"I cannot turn back," said Savitri. "I am obedient to Dharma, which dictates fidelity and obedience and friendship with the strict. I am not afraid to follow the path of a just ruler such as yourself, the King of Dharma. From you, I can expect the truth, nobility of mind and conduct."

Yama was surprised to hear such wisdom but still attempted to dissuade her.

"The path is not for you," he said. "It is the destiny of Satyavan to die today."

"I will not turn back," said Savitri, and repeated her words as they were before.

"Take any boon, then," said Yama, and added quickly, "save that of Satyavan's life."

"I have but three wishes, great Yama," said Savitri. "First, restore the sight and kingdom of Dyumatsena, for he lives in accordance with Dharma. Second, grant him a hundred children for my father, to carry on the name of his line. Third, grant me and my husband, Satyavan, a hundred children, that I may be compensated for his loss."

Then Yama was trapped, for how could he grant this boon without returning the life of Satyavan?

"Very well," he said. "This boon, since you asked in wisdom and fidelity, shall be granted."

Then Yama returned Satyavan's soul and honored Savitri for her courage and dedication. When Satyavan awoke, Savitri cradled him in her arms, crying, and told him the whole story. Their tears mingled, and they offered tapasya to both Brahma and Vishnu.

Thus Savitri saved her husband through fidelity and wisdom and petitioned Yama, the god of the dead.

Chapter 28: Chitragupta Takes Notes

Lord Brahma, the creator, went one day to visit Yama, the god of the dead. Lord Brahma passed the hounds that guarded the road, and their heads bowed to do him homage. He passed the buffalo, tethered in its pasture, upon which Yama rode through the earth. At length, he passed a line of waiting souls.

"What are you waiting for, souls of men?" asked Lord Brahma.

"For the judgment of Yama," they answered.

Lord Brahma continued down the line. He passed more souls, tall and short, lanky and robust.

"What are you waiting for, souls of men?" he asked.

"For the judgment of Yama," they answered.

Lord Brahma walked faster and faster until he reached the judgment seat of Yama.

"Good day, Yama," he said. "I have come to pay you a visit."

"To Swas," said Yama, with a bow.

"What?" said Lord Brahma, surprised. Yama shook his head.

"Not you. The souls. I send them to the swarga, the heaven, they need. There is no one else to judge and assign them."

"To Swas," said Yama again, and a soul passed onto the path that would take it to the realm of Indra.

Lord Brahma looked at the line of human souls awaiting judgment; it stretched out of his sight. Yama greeted the next soul and began the review of the soul's doings, good and bad. Yama reviewed the soul's actions, the reverences it made, and the tapasyas it performed. He reviewed its thoughts, its goings and comings, and doings of every day of its life. Finally, the review was finished.

"To Tharus," said Yama, and turned to the next soul. Lord Brahma saw the lines on Yama's brow and heard the shuffle of the souls waiting to receive judgment.

"Yama, is there no other way to judge the dead?" he asked.

"I was the first mortal who died, and thus assumed the burden of rule of the dead," said Yama. "Who else might assist me in my work?"

Lord Brahma thought, and from his thought sprung Chitragupta. Immediately Chitragupta took out his pen and a leaf and began to write more quickly than a gazelle in the field.

"Farmer, yes. Good father, yes. Did not honor Shiva, no. Offended a Rishi, no. Recommended for Bhuvas."

"Agreed," said Yama, and the soul started on its path. With Chitragupta's help, the line sped more quickly. Chitragupta studied the lives of men, recording their doings with his pen and leaf. When the time came to recommend them to one of the swargas or to return them to Bhoomi, the earth, Chitragupta had the summaries of each soul ready. He knew whether to send them deeper into Naraka to expiate sins or to send them to Maha, the swarga governed by Brahma himself. He knew the gateway to Thaarus and the formula for a good life and etched them on his records. Then Yama was pleased and thanked Lord Brahma for his help.

Thus became Chitragupta, who summarizes the lives of mortal men and recommends them for heaven.

Chapter 29: Ashes to Ashes

Bhasmasura sought a boon from Shiva. He performed tapasya and waited on Parvati for many years. He fasted and subjected himself to the elements. At last Lord Shiva heard his prayers.

"What boon do you seek from me, Bhasmasura?" he asked.

"Oh great Lord," Bhasmasura answered. "I wish to be as the ashes that cover your sacred flesh. Grant that whomever I touch on the head with my hands shall burn to ashes, that all might become sacred as you are."

"Let it be done," said Shiva. Then the eyes of Bhasmasura glinted with guile.

"Then come, great Lord," he said, "and turn to ashes yourself. For only when you are gone may I possess your wife, Parvati, and worship her as forcefully as I have desired."

Then Bhasmasura pursued Shiva, trying to touch him with his hands. Shiva raced through the forests and across the deserts, but Bhasmasura pursued him still. Finally, Shiva fell before Vishnu and begged his help.

"The demon Bhasmasura seeks my life and my wife," Shiva cried. "He uses my boon against me, and I will be turned to ashes."

Vishnu changed his form to Mohini, the beautiful enchantress. He danced in the path of Bhasmasura, drawing the demon's attention from Shiva.

"Marry me, Mohini," said Bhasmasura, mesmerized by her dance. "My heart and hand yearn after you."

"I will marry none but him who loves to dance as much as I," said Mohini, laughing. "Can you mimic my movements and prove yourself a proper husband?"

Bhasmasura, blinded by desire, agreed. When Mohini twirled, so did he. He followed her bharatanatyam and swayed through the symbols of odissi. They danced for many days until Bhasmasura lost suspicion and thought only of the beautiful Mohini and gaining her to wife. At last, Mohini twirled to finish, placing her hand on her head. After dancing for so long, Bhasmasura forgot Shiva's boon and placed his hand on his head.

Poof! Bhasmasura turned to ashes.

Thus Shiva was saved by the interference of Vishnu and learned to be more wary of his gifts.

If you enjoyed this individual book on Hindu mythology, can you please leave a review for it?

Thanks for your support!

Sources

Chinese Mythology:

Birrel, Anne (1999), Chinese Mythology: An Introduction.

Chew, Katherine Liang (2002), Tales of the Teahouse Retold: Investiture of the Gods.

Walters, Derek (1995), An Encyclopedia of Myth and Legend: Chinese Mythology.

Wilkinson, Philip (2011), Myths and Legends.

Yang, Lihui and An Deming, with Jessica Anderson Turner (2005), Handbook of Chinese Mythology.

Websites:

Worldstories.org.uk

www.shenyunperformingarts.org

https://en.wikisource.org/wiki/Portal:Investiture_of_the_Gods/

Japanese Mythology:

http://www.jinjahoncho.or.jp/en/image/soul-of-japan.pdf

https://library.uoregon.edu/ec/e-asia/read/kojiki.pdf

https://www.enotes.com/topics/kojiki

http://www.sacred-texts.com/shi/kj/index.htm

http://qcpages.qc.cuny.edu/~mfujimoto/EAST%20251/Handbook%20of%20Mythology%20intro1.pdf

https://books.google.com/books?id=gqs-y9R2AekC&pg=PA306&lpg=PA306&dq=michael+ashkenazi+japanese+mythology+read+online&source=bl&ots=Q00I43jxfh&sig=kRxVjkiB1ZMXf63PiODzHswJRJM&hl=en&sa=X&ved=2ahUKEwiw_YqP-4zZAhXRhOAKHQoCB0k4ChDoATANegQIERAB#v=onepage&q=michael%20ashkenazi%20japanese%20mythology%20read%20online&f=false

http://folklorethursday.com/legends/three-evil-yokai-japan/#sthash.Ue7TT11z.dpbs

http://yokai.com/about/

https://en.wikipedia.org/wiki/Toriyama_Sekien

http://nihonshoki.wikidot.com/

http://www.univie.ac.at/rel_jap/k/images/0/03/Kuroda_1981.pdf

https://www.gutenberg.org/files/4018/4018-h/4018-h.htm

Hindu Mythology

Chatterjee, Debjani. *The Elephant-Headed God and Other Hindu Tales*. Oxford University Press, 1992.

Doniger O'Flaherty, Wendy. *Hindu Myths: A Sourcebook Translated from Sanskrit*. Penguin Books, 1994.

Dowson, John. *A Classical Dictionary of Hindu Mythology and Religion, Geography, History, and Culture*. DK Printworld, 2014.

Egenes, Linda and Kumunda Reddy. *The Ramayana: A New Retelling of Valmiki's Ancient Epic—Complete and Comprehensive*. TarcherPerigree, 2016.

Mathur, Suresh Narain and B.K. Chaturvedi. *The Diamond Book of Hindu Gods and Goddesses: Their Hierarchy and Other Holy Things*. Diamond Pocket Books, 2005.

Murray, Alexander S. *The Manual of Mythology: Greek and Roman, Norse and Old German, Hindoo and Egyptian Mythology*. Newcastle Publishing, 1993.

Patel, Sanjay. *Ramayana: Divine Loophole*. Chronicle Books, 2010.